THE ME GENERATION...BY ME
(GROWING UP IN THE '60s)

First Edition: June 2012

THE ME GENERATION...BY ME
(GROWING UP IN THE '60s)

By
Ken Levine

For Marilyn & Clifford Levine – the parents of the decade.

Contents

INTRO.....Page 1

PART ONE.....Page 5

Duck and Recover • Oh Great! I've Got to Compete with the Beatles! • The Fifth Beatle • Meet the Levines and the Petries • A Typical Day and Dana in theLife • Vote for Me and Smoke • "The Ann Nauseda Story" • TV Land of 1000 Dances • The Fountain of Misspent Youth • West San Jacinto Side Story • I Did It Amway • You Never Forget Your First Whore • Woodland Hills Weed • Hard Day's Nukes • LBJ and Gypsy Boots

PART TWO......Page 63

Kind of a Drag • Nuns, Nazis, and Sex Education • Will Sitcoms Make You Go Blind? • Tina Delgado is Alive! Alive! • She's So Fine • Watts Happening • The Sunset Strip • Get Out of the Street! • Could the Tribe Keep It Down? • Be True To Your School • The End of the '50s • Before POW Meant Prisoner of War • You Don't Say • WKRP In Woodland Hills • The Meanest and Ugliest Teacher in the School • Working With an Ocelot and a Cricket • In Other News • The Big Kahuna •Hey, Hey, They're the Monkees

PHOTO SECTION......Page 127

PART THREE......Page 131

French Girls • There Goes My Career As a Mechanic • And the Hits Just Keep On Coming • It Was a Very Goodyear • Kiss the Rubber Chicken • Improbable Victories • The Return of Ann • The Return of Dana • Mr. Satisfy • Eleanor, You're My Pride & Joy, et cetera • On the Line with Cliff Levine • Vote For Me... Or Not • Don't Drink and Watch Plays • Flower Power! • Thanks for signing my yearbook • Love & Haight • The Semester of Rachel Salberg • What I Did For the Slim Hope of Sex • America's Rebels: The Smothers Brothers • Dear Applicant • In The Hour of Not Quite Rain • New Year's Revelation • Make Up Petting • The Graduate

PART FOUR......Page 223

At Least Clyde Got Laid • The Stamp Club Or the Black Panthers? • The Mighty KLA • The Unthinkable • My Radio Debut That No One Heard – Thank God • And Finally...Robert F. Kennedy • The Summer Of My Discontent • Both Sides Now • The Fall of America • Apostles of Non Violence Racial Harmony... and other Terrorists • If You Can't Beat Them... Beg Them For a Job • The Greatest Goldie Hawn Story Ever • These Are the Good Old Days • What If God Were One of Us? • Driving Miss Zsa Zsa • Tripping • We Did It!! • Helter Skelter • Help Me Rhonda • Woodstock • Woody • For Better, Four Worse • The Return of Rachel • The End of the '60s

ACKNOWLEDGEMENTS......Page 315

ABOUT THE AUTHOR......Page 317

INTRO

They say if you can remember the '60s you didn't live through them. But that's not true. 99.9999% of the largest generation the world has ever known grew up in the '60s and were not so drugged out that the decade became a mere purple haze. 99.999999% of them didn't attend Woodstock, move to Haight-Ashbury, protest the war by burning their bras or banks, or form a band that played Woodstock. Most of us went to school, had summer jobs, wrestled with adolescence, and enjoyed being catered to by the media and Madison Avenue because of our sheer size.

And the world changed dramatically while all of this was going on. But in the background.

Meanwhile, I set out on a journey to find myself and my place in the world set against the most confusing decade of the century. At the time, however, I didn't know it was a journey. I just thought it was life.

Books on the '60s generally read like history timelines. (SPOILER ALERT) "Camelot," then JFK is killed, then the Beatles, then the war, then hippies, then college protests, then more assassinations, then Woodstock, then we land on the moon. The final exam is Tuesday. Please review Chapters 5-12.

Films on the '60s all have the same tired storyline. Clean-cut All-American kid smokes one joint, moves to San Francisco and becomes either a hippie or college revolutionary. Throw in long hair, goofy costumes, and a Jefferson Airplane soundtrack and you've distilled the entire decade into ninety minutes.

What seems missing is an account of what it was really like growing up in this most amazing and turbulent period. The problem of course, is that there is no one story. You have 76,000,000 people all with unique experiences. I'm sure a high school quarterback's book would be very different from mine. How can he get enough rest for the big game when all these girls are calling him night and day? I have no idea what that world was like. Nor do I know what attending schools with separate drinking fountains for whites and blacks was like. Or having to shovel snow to get to class. Or coming home to a broken home. I grew up in Los Angeles, two parents, one brother, Jewish, uncoordinated, insecure, cynical, ambitious, weird. This is *my*story. I can't guarantee it's the most definitive account of the '60s but I promise you this – it's 100% candid and 85% accurate, give or take a few details.

Unlike actress Marilu Henner, I do not have the ability to remember what I had for lunch every day I've been alive. Nor did I keep a daily journal during the period in question. As you'll see, who had the time? Or was that anal? So to help reconstruct my life, I went to many sources. School transcripts, my high school yearbooks, numerous interviews with friends, family, faculty, and classmates, invaluable websites like mrpophistory.com, various '60s -themed groups on Facebook, magazines, tapes of radio broadcasts, family slides, screening period movies, and a fairly good memory although not Marilu Henner's.

And then there was the music. All kids listened to the radio. I practically had mine surgically implanted. I was so into the hits of that era that I memorized every song, artist, and record label. And worse—I still retain that information to this day. Can Marilu Henner do that? This useless skill has come in very handy since I associate people and events with specific songs. So it was very easy to crosscheck when the tunes were on the charts and construct a fairly accurate timeline.

I've changed the names of many of the people in this book. This allowed me to be as honest as I could while still sparing the subjects' feelings. Who isn't mortified when they think back to things *they* said or did when they were 14? I shall let them cringe in peace.

So I invite you to join me on my journey (now that I realize I was on one) through this most exciting decade. Along the way you'll encounter JFK, and Vietnam, and the peace marches. And also bomb shelters, teen sex, lack of teen sex, the draft, the Monkees, dress codes, Batman, cheerleaders, malls, the space race, water pipes, SATs, LSD, ROTC, SDS, CBS, NBC, ABC, WABC, KHJ, UCLA, FM, underground FM, acne, driving lessons, the generation gap, the credibility gap, *Gidget*, transistor radios, rabbit ears, Mustangs, Motown, ideals, Sonny & Cher, Sonny Liston, sunny California, storm troopers on the roof, Beatlemania, the Sunset Strip, 007, 1A, 4F, 45's, Wolfman, the Man From Uncle, Uncle Sam, Hanoi Jane, Mr. Clean, Mr. Ed, Ed Sullivan, dancers in cages, undercover narcs, Love Ins, Drive Ins, *the Dating Game*, the World's Fair, the lottery, Coppertone, Koufax, theater-in-the-round, student stand-bys, The *Fugitive*, John Wooden, Woody Allen, nose jobs, summer jobs, angst, joy, anger, and boredom.

The Me Generation... By Me looks back but also forward. What happened to those ideals? That youth? That attention? The times, they have a' changed.

Personally, I loved growing up in the '60s. Hopefully after reading my account of it, you will too.

Ken Levine
Los Angeles, Ca.
May 2012

PART ONE

Duck and Recover

The decade was almost half over before it really began. Before November 22, 1963 when President John Kennedy was assassinated in Dallas we were still living in the '50s. "The Greatest Generation" (as author/NBC News anchor/Letterman guest Tom Brokaw called it) came home in 1945 from the war anxious to begin their lives and partake in as much of the American Dream as their G.I. loans would let them.

They bought affordable tract homes in the suburbs by day and knocked up their wives by night. 76,000,000 American children were born between 1945 and 1964. At least half of them intended. The "greatest" generation spawned the largest generation that the world had ever known.

And I was one of them. Born in 1950, the world I entered was one of peacetime, prosperity, innocence, and order. Well... not peacetime *exactly*. We were in the middle of the Cold War and lived under the constant fear that Russia might drop a hundred-megaton nuclear bomb on our head at any minute and wipe us off the planet. So there was *that*.

Several nervous homeowners built bomb shelters. These were basements fortified with walls thick enough to withstand radiation. Grab a few cans of Dinty Moore chili, a Monopoly game, and a keg and in theory, your family could survive a nuclear blast for five or six years. They had it all figured out except what the *all-clear* signal was.

As proof of our staggering innocence we bought into the government's "Duck and Cover" campaign. If we just got under our desks or put a comic book over our heads when outside, we could easily survive a direct hit nuclear blast. Upon closer examination, in October of 1962 when the U.S. and U.S.S.R. went to the very brink of World War III, crouching under a table didn't seem sufficient. For a nervous week the notion of full-scale nuclear warfare seemed no longer just a possibility but imminent. I was twelve. I was going to die at twelve. What did I ever do to the Soviet Union?

When Russian Premier Nikita Khrushchev blinked first and backed off, the world heaved a collective sigh. I recovered by watching TV that night (Finally! The shows were back!), and when a promo came on for the *Perry Como Kraft Music Hall* on Wednesday my heart leaped with joy. I was going to be alive to see it! Of course I *didn't* see it. Who watches that shit? But make no mistake, that was a near-death experience and they stay with you. Even if you're too young to stay up past 10:00.

As a generation we sought answers, tried to make sense of the confusion that followed in the '60s. But there was always unease. Would we eventually "see the light?" Or "see the *blinding* light?"

Beyond that, in the '50s and early '60s I was just a kid. I played with toys, collected baseball cards, drew cartoons, and watched probably ten thousand hours of bad television. I didn't care about my future or the news. There was a Dodger game on the radio to listen to or a new Batman comic to buy at Van's Variety on Ventura. Only the shows, toys, players, and villains changed.

In 1961, President Kennedy delivered an electrifying inaugural address. It's the famous "Ask not…" speech. Also in that address he talks about "the torch being passed to a new generation."

Uh, he meant *us*!

On the one hand, that's very stirring and empowering, but on the other – what a huge burden to place on millions of kids who were still playing with Barbies and Strat-o-Matic Baseball.

So we had that weighing on us – the responsibility to safeguard and better the world – along with living under the constant dark (mushroom) cloud of complete incineration.

Then President Kennedy got shot.

Then the man who shot President Kennedy got shot.

Then adolescence arrived.

Now you've got a decade.

Oh Great! I've Got to Compete With the Beatles!

It's bad enough I grew a foot in my thirteenth year and weighed less than a plastic lawn flamingo. I was still reeling from a shattered love affair (well, *I* was in love, she had no idea) and only beginning puberty. Girls became my singular focus. On the night President Kennedy was shot I took time out from grieving to ogle photos of actress Diane Baker in a *LOOK* magazine layout. But *getting* girls – while clueless and looking like a Q-Tip with eyes – that was a near impossible task.

And then the Beatles appeared on *The Ed Sullivan Show*.

It was Sunday night, February 9, 1964.

At the time I didn't *know* they were a threat. Like everyone else I was curious to see them. They had first burst upon the scene a month before. It seemed like every hour a new Beatles song was premiering on Color Radio, KFWB. "I Want to Hold Your Hand." "Love Me Do." "She Loves You." They even started playing German versions ("Sie Liebt Dich"). That's when you knew you had a phenomenon on your hands (although German versions of Nazi anthems would be better than the Bobby Vinton schmaltzfests that were topping the charts back then).

I was almost 14, living in a ranch style tract home in an upper middle class suburb of the San Fernando Valley called Woodland Hills. I was part of the ideal American Dream family unit – two parents, two children (picture Ozzie & Harriet but with Jews).

Back in 1964 there were only three networks and we watched whatever crap was on. Human-robot Ed Sullivan hosted a weekly variety show tolerated by the entire family. I can't tell you how many three-legged dog acts and Szony & Claire dance teams I suffered through just to catch three minutes of the Four Seasons or dancer Abby Lane in leotards.

The Beatles' timing couldn't have been better. The country was still in a giant funk over JFK and we needed something to lift us out of the doldrums. But why couldn't it have been a *girl* group?

I was already a little skeptical. Beatles songs were fine but this was Southern California. We already *had* our group – The Beach Boys. They connected with *our* lives and *our* lifestyle. The beach, surfing, hot cars, that whole California dream. It was *real!* We were living it. Okay, well, *I* wasn't living it. I don't think I could lift a surfboard at that age. And beach bunnies seemed more impressed with Corvettes than Schwinn ten-speed bicycles with raised handlebars.

But that was unimportant. The Beach Boys were singing *our* anthems. "Surfin' USA," "Surfin' Safari," or the one I identified with, "In My Room" – where you locked out all your worries and fears by retreating to your cell.

In my room Ann loved me. If only she loved me anywhere else.

So I watched the Beatles that Sunday night. Me, and 72,999,999 other folks. They were dazzling, electric; unlike anything I'd ever seen. Words can't explain why. You look at the footage today and it's just four English guys with surprisingly decent teeth in matching dark suits and helmet hair bouncing around singing "Yeah yeah yeah" in harmony, but I could sense, right then, that something big was happening. I could just feel it. Not just big, but huge, seismic – a national coming out party for my generation.

The start of a revolution!

My euphoria lasted maybe thirty seconds because then I saw all the girls in the audience. They were being driven to complete madness. Shrieking and crying, and practically throwing their training bras onto the stage. What the hell? I had never seen *this* either.

The Fifth Beatle

The next morning, Parkman Jr. High, where I was trapped in the 9th grade, was abuzz with the Beatles. That's all anyone talked about at "Nutrition." (Why they called this recess "Nutrition" I do not know. The only items they sold were flying saucer sugar cookies and chocolate milk.) The girls in particular were nuts. They'd cluster in excited little huddles, debating over which Beatle was cuter, squealing and laughing. I was doomed.

My best friend, Gary McMahon observed, "We're never going to get laid." "It's worse," I said. "I'm going to be in the Corbin Theater one night and there will be Ann sharing an Abba Zabba bar with Ringo Starr." (Jesus, what a drama queen!)

Every boy tried to wear his hair like a Beatle. It wasn't easy since we all had crewcuts. Combing it down over our foreheads we looked more like Julius Caesar than Paul McCartney.

But the message was clear:

If you want to get girls, be a rock star.

That afternoon every cheap guitar in America was purchased along with every "How to" book and piece of Beatles sheet music. I imagine some guys were so desperate they began taking German lessons.

I didn't want to expend the time, effort, and money required to buy and learn how to play the guitar, but fortunately I found a faster, easier, and cheaper way to achieve the same ultimate goal. I bought a $5 harmonica.

John Lennon had played harmonica on "Love Me Do." It was an *official* Beatles instrument. And it came with a three-page booklet teaching you how to use it. Forget that the instructions were in Japanese.

So like an idiot, I would come home from school, lock myself (and my worries and fears) in my room, and blow into this crappy piece of tin till I had a hernia. Little did I know, not even Polka bands wanted a harmonica player.

I didn't become a rock star. My goal was that by the end of the '60s I'd become *something*. I'd define myself and my place in the world. But honestly, of greater importance was seeing a vagina just once before I died.

The Beatles appeared on *The Ed Sullivan Show* again the next week, but this time instead of playing to frenzied teenage girls in New York, they performed in Miami Beach for old Jews. The electricity just wasn't the same singing for codgers in leisure suits with hearing aids who show their appreciation by clicking spoons. Charlie Brill & Mitzi McCall received a bigger ovation.

Like kids everywhere, we followed the group's U.S. exploits through the radio. Every Top 40 station in the country covered it, and every one seemed to have one D.J. who crowned himself "the fifth Beatle." Yeah, like the Beatles were going to let only *one* person into their inner circle and it was going to be some pimple cream huckster from Yakima. Murray "the K." Kaufman in New York was the most outspoken "fifth Beatle," but in Los Angeles it was Dave "the Hullabalooer" Hull. Dave did afternoons on KFWB's chief rival, KRLA. He led his audience to believe that he and the boys were BFF's (Beatles' Fifth Forever). If Dave needed a kidney, George Harrison would *insist* he take his.

According to Dave, the Beatles had slipped into Los Angeles and were hiding out in a secluded mansion somewhere in Bel Air. I'm sure after his show Dave was going to go up there and maybe flip some burgers for the guys (unless the "fifth Beatle" from Kalamazoo got there first).

I was visiting a friend, Bobby Celina, who lived in Bel Air and he had heard that the Beatles were staying with Capitol Records President, Alan Livingston, whose estate was right up the street. "Great!" I thought, "I can tell Ringo Starr to keep his limey hands off Ann." So we decided to go up there and meet 'em. I guess we should've thought the plan through a little further, but time was a'wastin'. Off we hiked up to Livingston's house.

Here's one of those little details we should have worked out first: exactly *which* house was Livingston's. Bobby knew it was one of like six but couldn't say for sure which one.

We decided to go around to the alley, climb fences, scope out backyards and try to surmise which was Location X. Maybe we'd get lucky and spot the Fab Four catching some rays or playing Marco Polo in the pool with Elvis.

We never saw the Beatles that day. We did see a fat lady sitting on a lounge chair. Unfortunately, she saw us. She screamed and her Mexican maid tore after us for a block. So much for my illusions of becoming the next James Bond. A five-foot Chihuahua with an apron had sufficiently scared the shit out of me.

There's no chance we *would* have seen the Beatles. Despite the "fifth Beatles" inside knowledge, they were already back in London by then.

In later years I did meet John Lennon, passed George Harrison on the street once, and Ringo almost hit me with his car.

But by then they were just people.

Meet the Levines and the Petries

I know this is a very un-'60s thing to say but I never rebelled against my parents.

Yes, there was the issue of smoking and drinking but they were the ones who smoked and drank. I was never embarrassed by my folks, appalled by their value system, or at odds with their religious beliefs. I hated that my father made me mow the lawn and pull weeds with him every Saturday morning, but that's not like being forced into Scientology.

My brother Corey is four years younger. He was ten in 1964 and much more your regular kid. He wanted to *be* a ballplayer, not the guy describing his at-bat and reminding you that, "*an ice cold glass of Blatz beer sure would go good right about now.*" We fought as most brothers did, usually over vital issues like who had to sit in the back of the Impala. But neither of us ever sent the other to the Emergency Room so I guess we really did love each other. Blood is thicker than blood.

Cliff & Marilyn Levine were in their mid 30s in 1964. But they could have been in their 40s or 80s, it made no difference. They were "adults." And as a teenager you swing back and forth between thinking they know everything and nothing. Generally I gave them the benefit of the doubt. They were hands-on parents who clearly loved us, cared about our well-being, and in my case, tolerated a weird kid who—once he shed blissful childhood—was insecure about his looks, his weight, his voice, and didn't know whether he wanted to be a baseball announcer, screaming disc jockey, *New York Times* theatre caricaturist, *Tonight Show* host, Broadway playwright, James Bond (sorry, strike that one), Looney Tunes animator, or Rob Petrie.

Rob Petrie was the character Dick Van Dyke played in *The Dick Van Dyke Show*. Rob was a comedy writer, worked with zany cohorts, lived in a sprawling suburban house, and best of all was married to "Laura." Sweet, sexy, adorable Laura, as played by the then-sweet, sexy, adorable Mary Tyler Moore, was my fantasy of the absolute perfect woman. And if a comedy writer could marry a girl like that then maybe there was hope for me. Of course, Rob Petrie was also good-looking, and could sing and dance.

My parents socialized with other couples, went out Saturday nights, played weekly card games and in general were far more youthful and active than parents I saw on TV. My dad never wore a tie around the house, my mother never put on a dress to bake a meat loaf. Every night my father would come home from work and they'd have a cocktail together at the kitchen table. Nick & Nora Charles go suburban. We always ate dinner together as a family. We never said grace but did have occasional whipped cream fights. For dessert one night my mom presented a bowl of strawberries and two aerosol cans of Reddi Whip. I don't know who started it. Probably Dad. But within minutes whipped cream was flying in all directions. We were a dysfunctional family in a good way.

Our parents had us early. Prior to me, my mother was one of the first TV models. They'd break away from Ben Hunter's "Mid-day

Movie" on KTTV, Channel 11 and there was my mom pointing out fine china settings, which you could order by calling the number on your screen. I like to think my mother blazed the trail for Vanna White.

She didn't go back to work post-me, preferring to be a stay-at-home housewife. That was the status quo in the '50s. Then a book came along in 1963 called *The Feminine Mystique* by Betty Friedan that made some shocking revelations. Laura Petrie and Betty Draper apparently felt unfulfilled spending their lives relegated to the role of maids. Who knew? Apparently not Rob Petrie and Don Draper. This book was a bombshell and sparked what became Feminism – women taking more control of their lives, following *their* passions, and busting out of roles just dictated by society. Mom however, seemed genuinely content just staying home raising two kids. We must've been adorable children; that's the only explanation I can possibly think of.

My father sold air. More specifically, air *time*. He was a radio station air time salesman. He worked for KRKD, a station that played Sinatra during the day, then horse racing results, religion in the evening, and Polynesian music all night. They appealed to that large Hawaiian-Christian-Gambler-Hipster crowd.

KRKD was owned by the Angelus Temple, founded by flamboyant preacher Aimee Semple McPherson in the 1920s. L.A. just seems to attract these nut jobs. As proof of her healing abilities she had a wheelchair and crutch museum in her church. Ms. McPherson is best known for faking her own abduction in 1926, banging some married employee in a motel while her loyal parishioners kept day and night vigils. She probably violated six Commandments with that one stunt.

When the station wasn't praising Jesus or Seabiscuit it billed itself as "the Album Station" playing middle-of-the-road artists like

Frank, Tony, Sammy, Steve & Eydie, and of course Pat Suzuki. As a result, when the station received promo copies of 45 RPM singles they would just toss them into a box and Dad would bring them home for me. It was great. In only two years I had amassed the largest collection of non-hits in the entire world!! Friends would come over after school and we would listen to them in horror and amusement. One of those friends was Mike Monarch. He went on a few years later to record some songs himself. But they weren't flops. Mike Monarch became the lead guitarist of Steppenwolf. I'd like to think that sitting in my room, absorbing Neil Sedaka singing "Alice in Wonderland" inspired him to go off and do "Goddamn the Pusher Man."

I look back at my relationship with my parents with great fondness. I can honestly say I'm in therapy for *other* reasons. Key parental memories of 1964 besides being blinded with whipped cream: Coming home from school and playing gin rummy with my mom. Going to Dodger games with my dad.

Getting to those games was an adventure. Since Dad worked downtown and I couldn't drive, I would take a city bus from Ventura Blvd. all the way east through the valley and down to the corner of Hollywood & Vine in Hollywood. It took an hour-and-a-half. There I would wait for another 15 minutes or so until Dad drove up and off we'd go. The amazing thing was – you could *do* that in 1964. It was actually *safe*. A 14-year-boy could stand at Hollywood & Vine without being peed on, mugged by a crack-head, checked out by two drag queens, flashed by some pervert, propositioned by a 50-year-old hooker, or asked directions to the Frederick's of Hollywood Museum of Bras by some tourist.

Dodger Stadium was a magical place for me. Brand new, modern in its wedding cake design, and for three hours I could just lose myself in the world in baseball. I never cared where I sat. Just being there was a thrill. Gorging on bad hot dogs, keeping score of every pitch, and actually seeing in person the likes of Hank Aaron, Stan Musial, Willie Mays, Roberto Clemente, Bob Gibson, Ernie Banks, and Choo Choo Coleman. These men were larger-than-life figures to me even though from up where I was sitting they were just ants. And to be sharing it all with my father made it all the more special.

My favorite photo of my parents was taken in 1964. It was my dad's 20th high school reunion. They look so vibrant, so happy, so clearly in love with each other. It's hard to rebel against people you hope to become.

A Typical Day and Dana in the Life

The clock radio goes off at 6:30 with one of the ten current Beatles hits. I curse, shower, and dress. There was a strict dress code in the LA Unified School District. Collared shirts, tucked in, long pants – no jeans. Skirts for girls. My usual outfit was a white shirt, dark pants, and sweater buttoned up to my nose.

And my thick glasses complimented the ensemble *perfectly*.

There were two gangs (in the loosest form of the word) at Parkman – the Surfers and the Greasers. Surfers tended to wear flannel Pendleton shirts and Greasers (car enthusiasts) wore leather. On rare occasions they would fight under the freeway bridge (over what I do not know. Waves are better than drag strips? Who gives a shit?). I was in neither gang. I associated with no one in either gang. Wearing sweaters usually signified guys who spent a lot of time in their rooms.

I gulped my daily glass of *Carnation Instant Breakfast* (summer was coming and I wanted to be up to 131 pounds, maybe even 132) while perusing the sports section. LA had two major newspapers – the *Times* and the less popular *Examiner*. Since the *Times* wouldn't hire my late grandfather to be a typesetter in the early '40s, our family refused to give those rat bastards a dime. We always subscribed to the *Examiner*. That was fine with me. Better sports section. The *Times* had the superior news bureau, but so what? What kid reads the news?

We now had Grandpappy in the White House. LBJ might become a great president but he wasn't JFK. Starlet Angie Dickinson never hopped into the sack with Lyndon Johnson. There were reports that we were sending more "advisors" to somewhere called Vietnam, but that was still pretty much under the radar.

The only story I was really following was the Frank Sinatra Jr. kidnapping case. Imagine someone trying to get back at the Corleone family by abducting Fredo. The three nimrods who pulled off this harebrain scheme were found guilty by a federal jury and sentenced to life plus 75 years, which is still getting off easier than if Frank had doled out justice *his way*. My interest was really sparked because the buffoons' hideout was just a few blocks from my house. It's the kind of national attention new tract housing developments could only *dream* about.

I took a city bus to school and back. I'd wait on Ventura Blvd. in front of Babe's Bar, which already had four or five pickled tosspots at 7:20 AM. To save some money (fifty whole cents!) I would often hitchhike home. It was either safer times or I'm lucky I'm not in seven mason jars in some nut's basement.

Parkman Jr. High was a typical single-story sprawling complex with just enough trees to differentiate it from a prison. If you've seen the original *Karate Kid*, it's like *that* school.

Everyone reported first to Homeroom where we heard school announcements for upcoming flu shots and Glee Club Hootenannies.

Off to English with Mr. Lucey. It was here I first wrote my book report for *The Great Escape*. I would continue to submit it all the way through college. It averaged a C+ at Taft High and a B at UCLA.

History followed with Mr. Sima. To force us to follow current events he gave a weekly quiz provided by those rat bastards at the *LA Times*. In preparation, I would watch the George Putnam newscast on KTTV, Channel 11. George was an L.A. institution and the inspiration for the blowhard Ted Baxter character on the *Mary Tyler Moore Show*. One night George looked straight into the camera, and bellowed in a booming voice, "Alan Ladd is DEAD!!!!"

"AAAAAAA!" I screamed and almost fell off the couch. George scared the shit out of me. And I didn't even know who Alan Ladd *was*. (He was a Hollywood actor, known for playing tough guys and short people.)

I did terrible on those quizzes. Unless the question was *"Alan Ladd is… A) Alive, B) Dead, C) DEAD!!!!!!!!!"* I retained nothing.

Next was "Nutrition" for our mid-morning wellness sugar fix, then on to Science with Mr. Romold. There was a certain relevance to this course. America was in the space race and nearby in the Santa Susana Mountains they were building the rockets. When we'd start hearing loud rumblings that almost felt like earthquakes, we knew we were only a month or two away from another NASA launch.

One feature our sleepy little suburban community had that others didn't was armed Nike and Hercules missiles vigilantly guarding our lawns and bird baths. This was still the Cold War and the defense plants that designed and built the new space age equipment were deemed potential targets. Bel Air had rent-a-cop patrol cars to keep it safe; Woodland Hills had thermal nuclear rockets.

Poor Mr. Romold was the target of one of my more asinine pranks. He had this fish tank with tropical fish that he doted on constantly. They received more attention than we did, which needless to say, was annoying. One day on the way to my desk I just casually dropped a root beer Fizzy into the tank. These were essentially flavored Alka-Seltzer tablets. A moment later it caught his eye – the swirl of brown bubbles – and he absolutely freaked out. He thought it was acid. For ten frantic minutes he scooped his beloved collection into tumblers, much to the delight of the other *school* in his charge. No, I was never caught. No, I was not proud of myself (but it was pretty damn funny). NOTE: *No fish were harmed in the execution of this stunt.*

Fourth period I had Typing. It was as close to a "shop" class as I would take. Handing me a soldering iron is like handing a monkey a gun.

At lunch I sat with my best friend, Gary. Daily topics would include the Dodgers, plot inconsistencies in Beach Party movies, how could brash upstart Cassius Clay beat Sonny Liston for the heavyweight title (the fix had to be in), Laura Petrie, music, and charting the daily progress of every girl's breast development. I think Gary still has the chart. I would mercilessly rag on the popular kids – how clueless and conceited and worthless they were – but deep down in my heart of hearts, I would've sold Gary to slave traders to be one of them.

Gary was a half-year ahead of me and was graduating in June. I would not be sprung until January. Back then, in L.A. public schools you could enter the system in mid-year (based on your birthday) and thus graduate mid-year. These were smaller classes, always out of sync with the usual school year of events. I was in one of those classes. *Winter Graduates* we were called, but I preferred the more accurate – *Left-Behinds.*

So I envied Gary. Jr. High was for babies. Sr. High was so much more "adult." You still couldn't drive, but you were *associating* with people who could!

After lunch was gym. It's the only class I ever got a "D" in, which takes some real effort. If you can do five jumping jacks, you're a valedictorian. And then there were…the showers. Nothing promotes homophobia and insecurity in a pre-teen like daily showers with your classmates. No guy would ever be caught dead checking out other guys. But we all did.

The very worst was saved for last. Math. Not because of equations or that thing where two trains leave the station and you have to figure out which one gets better steam mileage. It's because every time I walked into that classroom…

…there was Dana.

I was always in love with someone at that age (besides Ann of course, but she was gone and there's only so much of my mom's Sinatra a 14-year-old can process). In the 9th grade it was Dana Dellray. I was completely smitten by this little blond shiksa goddess. She was the perfect bronzed California Surfer Girl (except she never surfed, had alabaster skin, and was kind of a stuck-up bitch. But that combo worked for me).

I would occasionally muster up the courage to talk to her. Scintillating conversations about homework and… well, just pretty much homework. Dana was usually aloof, but I didn't know if that was personal to me or just her general raging bitchiness.

Two years earlier for Ann's birthday I had sent her a letter. Nothing too schmaltzy; I merely *suggested* that her coming into the world was comparable to the birth of the Christ child. Ann found my note very endearing and even wrote me back. I was ecstatic. Not only was it a personal thank you to me in her own cursive handwriting, it smelled like her perfume. Who needed naked pictures of women to get me aroused when I could just sniff an envelope?

Anyway, I figured why *tell* Dana how I felt about her in person and possibly trip on my tongue when I could just convey my feelings succinctly in a letter? I spent a good week crafting that masterpiece, rewriting it endlessly until every sentence was a work of art, every sentiment expressed with pinpoint perfection. Very proud of myself, I slipped it in her locker.

Big mistake. Big big big mistake.

The next day in class, not only did Dana snub me, she passed around my letter to all of her friends. Why didn't she just stuff my head in a wood chipper? That would have been quicker. I was the complete laughing stock of the 9th grade.

And how do you save face from something like that? (Today the letter would be posted on Facebook and girls in Malaysia would be laughing at me. So I guess I should be grateful.)

For weeks the snickering continued. Thank God Lenny King took the pressure off by being caught with Maiden Form bra ads in his binder.

I have never written another heartfelt love letter. Ever. To anyone. Not that that whole Dana experience left any lasting scars or anything.

My after school activities in March 1964 consisted of gearing up for the new Dodger season, rocking out on my harmonica, hanging with Gary and a few other chums, watching the *Dick Van Dyke Show* religiously (and perversely), listening to the latest flop records, and drawing comic books. My main character was a Don Quixote-like cartoon skunk (roughly in the style of Looney Tunes) who discovered what I firmly believed at the time—the only way to get women was to save their lives. *Pepe LeJew.*

Eventually, I graduated to caricatures, adopting a style very similar to the brilliant theatre caricaturist of the *New York Times*, Al Hirschfeld. How similar? He would always hide the name of his daughter, *Nina*, somewhere in every drawing. I hid the name *Dana.*

Vote For Me and Smoke

There were two big elections in 1964. The presidential and the more hotly contested "vice president of the student body" race at Parkman Jr. High. I was one of the candidates (of the latter). This was a way to maybe impress girls without having to pull them out of buildings about to explode.

At the time, Henry Cabot Lodge, Nelson Rockefeller, and the far scarier Barry Goldwater were duking it out in the Republican primaries while President Johnson was opening the World's Fair in New York. (The two big attractions were Michelangelo's Pieta and Walt Disney's "It's a Small Small World.")

My campaign for VP consisted of a poster, construction paper buttons, and a speech to be delivered to the entire student body. Every good campaign needs a great slogan and I had mine. Personally I thought it was way better than *All the way with LBJ* or Goldwater's *In your heart you know he's right*(in truth: *In your heart you know he's a fucking psycho who will start World War III*).

Mine was *Ken Satisfies Best,* which was a slight modification of Kent cigarettes very popular catchphrase *Kent Satisfies Best.* To stay with the theme I drew my poster to look like a package of Kent cigarettes.

My campaign was an immediate sensation. Everyone wanted to wear one of my buttons. Most people just added the "t" back to Kent and suddenly the campus was filled with minors advocating smoking.

The principal went ballistic. I was immediately expelled, and my buttons and posters were banned from the school.

After a day of my parents assuring the administration that my campaign was not underwritten by the Lorillard Tobacco Company—and that nowhere do I mention the benefits of the Micronite Filter—I was reinstated. But the damage to my campaign was irreparable. Cigarettes don't just kill people; they kill political careers, too!

"The Ann Nauseda Story"

LBJ continued to press for the Civil Rights Bill. Not a lot of blacks lived in Woodland Hills. The only place you really saw them was at the Hamburger Hamlet restaurant at Ventura & Topanga Canyon. The waiters were all African-Americans in formal jackets and vests. I never got the point. It was the antebellum burger joint? I remember being creeped-out, even then.

"Ringo for President" posters were everywhere. Would that make Ann the first lady? Stop it, I told myself. This is not helping.

Okay, who's Ann?

You probably know her.

The movie-of-the-week about her life is still one of the highest rated ever.

The Ann Jillian Story, or, as I knew her: *the Ann Nauseda Story*.

It's the first day of "Introduction to Music." 7th grade. A requirement. The teacher needed to know our strengths and limitations, so we were all assigned a song to sing in class the next day.

Every performance bordered on painful. If you were walking by the room, you probably thought we were giving a cat a bath. I was just about to stick an ice pick in my eye when this angelic voice filled the room. I looked up and the most beautiful girl I had ever seen was giving a bravura performance of "Somewhere Over the Rainbow." I was a goner. I didn't know at the time that this little goddess with a nondescript hair band and saddle shoes had already starred in *Gypsy* with Natalie Wood.

All I knew was that I was in love and even the humiliation of having to then follow her by massacring "Tumbling Tumbleweeds" did nothing to weaken my infatuation.

We became friends. More platonic than anything else, but when you're 12, what, you're going to get her all liquored up and book a room at Howard Johnson's?

In gym class on Fridays that year we had coed dancing. This went against thousands of years of my heritage because Jews don't square dance. While they were dosey-doeing in Kansas we were in Russia fleeing death squads. On the last week however, I heard we were to learn ballroom dancing. We'd be paired as couples, not groups of corn pones that didn't know their allemande left from their allemande ass. We entered the gym in two single file lines – the boys along one wall, girls along the opposite wall. I saw Ann come in and quickly figured out where she was in line. I then ran ahead and squeezed in between two guys. We all then walked to the center of the gym and what a coincidence, Ann was my partner.

Our graceful instructors, who otherwise coached football, told us how to stand then played "Georgia on my Mind" by Ray Charles. I took Ann in my arms, and if there's ever such a thing as a perfect moment – that one precious point in time you know you will cherish for the rest of your life – this was it. Holding her near, inhaling the tiny dab of perfume behind her ear – I was absolutely transformed. It was just dancing in a harshly lit sweaty gymnasium, and although I knew she really didn't have those feelings for me and that this was as intimate as our relationship would ever get, I didn't care. Not at that instant. I was in sheer ecstasy. Ann was mine... for three whole minutes.

That entire 7th Grade year I was on a cloud. We even went bowling twice!

From time to time she would be away for a month or so filming an episode of *Wagon Train* or the television classic – "Sammy, The Way Out Seal" for the Sunday night *Disneyland* program. Those were always long months and I never allowed myself to consider that she probably wasn't missing me (and if she thought of me at all it was when she had to dance with the seal), but she always returned and things went right back to normal.

And then one time they didn't.

She never returned. Her parents enrolled her in St. Mel's, a nearby Catholic school. I was devastated. Persuading my parents that St. Mel's wasn't *that* Catholic and I should transfer didn't really fly. Life was suddenly very empty. I'd come home everyday and just go to my room and draw dark comic books. The arch villain was always the Pope.

In time the pain for Ann began to subside. And the Dodgers sweeping the Yankees in the '63 World Series didn't hurt. I tried to keep in touch but it was hard. She was always going off to film a *Ben Casey* or *Twilight Zone* episode (So in addition to Ringo, I now had to worry about hunks like Vince Edwards and Rod Serling.) We eventually drifted apart but reconnected about thirty years ago and have remained friends ever since. My schoolboy crush has been replaced by enormous admiration for all she's accomplished and the inspiration she has selflessly given to others.

Anyway, I was determined to learn something from this experience. I would never make that same mistake – I would never again give my heart to someone I knew would never return my affections.

So my next crush was my teacher.

Miss. Perlman was probably 25. It's hard to tell with older women. I was 13 at the time. She taught Public Speaking. Yes, there was the slight age difference, but on the plus side, there was no religious conflicts and I never had to worry she'd go off for a month to film a *Gilligan's Island* episode. But she was engaged and I found that to be an obstacle I couldn't quite overcome by dazzling her with my speech on federal embargos.

So I would just gaze up at her in class, fantasizing about us both being naked, doing things I had only heard about—she calling out "Ohh Kennnny!" and me calling back "Ohhh Miss Perlmannnn!"

Still, I thank her for at least diverting my attention from Ann and serving as a nice transitional infatuation until my hormones were ready to move on. And once she told me to tuck in my shirt. So she had to be looking at my crotch.

TV Land of 1000 Dances

Must-viewing: *The Lloyd Thaxton Show*. Each afternoon from 5:00-6:00 Lloyd Thaxton hosted a live dance party show on the cheapest cheesiest independent station in LA – KCOP. If his budget was more than $4.95 a show I'd be shocked.

His set consisted of four panels (probably cardboard) with musical notes drawn on them. Kids from local high schools were invited to dance on a soundstage the size of an elevator. This was appointment television for every teenager in Los Angeles.

What made the show special was Lloyd Thaxton. Most shows like this were hosted by disc jockeys. They were content to just introduce the records and step aside while the kids did the Twist, Jerk, Fly, Popeye, Monkey, Frug, Mashed Potato, Locomotion, and whatever other inane dance was the rage that minute. Lloyd was the first to realize "this was TELEVISION," you had to do something VISUAL. So he would find ways to comically present the songs. This elfin redhead would lip sync, mime playing instruments, use finger puppets, don wigs, do duets with rubber masks, cut out the lips on an album cover and substitute his own – anything to make the songs fun. In many ways, Lloyd Thaxton was a local version of

Ernie Kovacs, finding innovative new ways to use the new medium. Music videos these days are all ambitious, elaborate productions. Back then we were quite content to watch a guy sing into his hand.

I always wanted to be on his show but of course didn't qualify because I was still in *Junior* High. The indignities continue! I did however, get to appear on *Ninth Street West*.

With the success of *The Lloyd Thaxton Show,* every local channel had their own dance party copycat. Over the next few years there would be *Shebang* on Channel 5 with Casey Kasem, *Shivaree* on Channel 7 with KFWB DJ, Gene Weed, and *Ninth Street West* on Channel 9 hosted by KFWB DJ, Sam Riddle. Stations hired the DJ's with the best and most teeth.

I sent in requests to all of them, but only *Ninth Street West* bit. Talk about a great date—taking a girl to a TV show and dinner at nearby Carolina Pine's coffee shop in Hollywood. Thanks again for driving, Mom!

I asked my friend Marcia. You always want to be seen on TV with someone hotter than you, but not so hot that it screams "pity date." Marcia was very cute yet believable as my escort.

The show originated from the Channel 9 studios on Melrose Ave. The soundstage was nothing more than a one-car garage (for a VW maybe). About forty of us were jammed into this tiny space. It's hard to rock out with reckless abandon when at any moment you could get an elbow in your eye.

There were several guests scheduled to lip sync their songs. It was impossible to perform live. One amplifier and ten dancers would be pinned against the wall. The guests that night were the Beau Brummels (a group out of San Francisco), and British imports, Peter & Gordon.

Kids were so crazed over the Beatles that they started buying records from any group that came out of England. It's the same principle where girls who can't sleep with rock stars wind up in bed with their roadies. First it was the Dave Clark 5, and then the floodgates opened. Billy J. Kramer and the Dakotas (who sang one of the creepiest songs EVER – "Little Children." The story of a guy threatening little children because they caught him diddling their sister. Ugh!), Gerry & the Pacemakers, Herman's Hermits, the inane Freddy & the Dreamers (whose entire act was to wear suits that didn't fit and do jumping jacks), and Peter & Gordon. The harder edged Rolling Stones, Animals, Who, and Lulu would come a bit later.

Also guesting on the show that night was a very young Marvin Gaye. During a commercial break they set up for his number. Surprisingly, he seemed incredibly nervous. His hands were practically shaking. I assured him he was great and had nothing to worry about. It must have meant a lot coming from a white kid in his bar mitzvah suit. He gave me a quick smile, the red light went on, and he did his song. Afterwards when he was off camera he thanked me. Not necessary, but a lovely gesture.

The next day in school Marcia was quite the celebrity. Everyone had seen her on *Ninth Street West*. Maybe two or three had seen me. I wanted to say, "Hey, screw you, people. *I'm* the one who saved Marvin Gaye's career!"

It was only a matter of time before the dance show craze went national. In the fall of '64, ABC premiered *Shindig*. This show featured more performers, more dancers (including a very young Teri Garr), and a full band (featuring anonymous musicians Glen Campbell, Billy Preston, and Leon Russell). I was almost there the night the pilot was taped.

See, I had made a new friend that year, Jon Solomon. Jon and his family had recently moved out from New Jersey. Jon's father owned jukeboxes. On Saturdays I would tag along with Jon as Mr. Solomon made the rounds, collecting the change from his various machines. We hit every *Bada Bing* bar in the valley. Wow, I thought, he must take in a lot of dimes to be able to afford a big house in Woodland Hills. It never occurred to me that jukeboxes, New Jersey – the guy was probably a gunsel for the mob! I drove around every Saturday with a bag man.

But he must've had real connections with record distributors because one day he announced he had tickets for the pilot taping of this new show, *Shindig.* Jon invited me. Mr. Solomon was working that night (probably delivering a horse head), so Jon's mom drove us. The taping was at ABC, which was in East Hollywood. Jon's mother was not yet not familiar with Los Angeles streets. Her directions said get off the Hollywood Freeway at Vermont. We did. But the directions didn't specify whether to then go left or right. I had no clue. When you're 14, people always drive you. I had no idea where anything was.

Mrs. Solomon turned right, and we kept going. And going. And going. We were starting to get the uneasy feeling we might have made a wrong turn. This was looking less and less like Hollywood. You rarely see a burning car in front of Grauman's Chinese Theater. A Jewish woman and two kids were now driving through the heart of Watts at night. (There was probably a gun in the glove compartment, but which one of us knew how to use it?) Not sure what the ultimate tip off was – the car in flames, the ramshackled houses, perhaps the absence of a single white face – but we finally realized this was not where the American Broadcasting Company chose to locate their Los Angeles headquarters.

I can't say we were panicked. But we were, uh… concerned. (Years later when I was announcing for the Seattle Mariners and we played in New York, we would take the team bus back to the hotel through Harlem. My broadcast partner, Dave Niehaus was sitting next to one of the African-American coaches, Vada Pinson. Dave said, "If this bus breaks down, you're my best friend" to which Pinson replied, "If this bus breaks down, I don't know you.")

We turned around and just headed home. Had we originally turned left on Vermont, we would have run into ABC in three blocks.

It was disappointing, but there have been a couple of nights over the years when my own pilots were being taped and I thought to myself, "I would sooo rather be in Watts."

The Fountain of Misspent Youth

The Topanga Plaza opened!

Finally! A place for teenagers to loiter in air-conditioned comfort!

The Topanga Plaza was L.A.'s first indoor mall. So take *that* West Covina and Terminal Island! It's one thing to just *call* yourself a great suburb, but now we had an Orange Julius, Montgomery Wards, and Morrow's Nuts to prove it! No wonder the Soviet Union viewed Woodland Hills as a target!

The mall was about the size of a city block; two tiered, flanked by Broadway and May Co. department stores with a "Monkey Wards" in the middle. There was also an ice-skating rink (a reminder that in other parts of the world they had this thing called "winter"), Don Paul's Seven Kitchens food court (many varieties of corn dogs), and the world's coolest fountain.

Beads of water (actually glycerin) ran down these ceiling-to-floor thin transparent plastic or nylon tubes creating a rainforest effect. When psychedelic drugs became fashionable a few years later this fountain became a big attraction. Just staring at it for ten hours became very commonplace.

On the opposite end of the mall there were kiosks with exotic birds and monkeys in large circular cages. That might not sound like a big deal but I don't know one kid who didn't love those monkeys.

However, the real attraction to anyone under 20 was Wallichs Music City record store. Owned by the ubiquitous Clyde Wallichs, his Music City stores were an L.A. institution. The main branch was at Sunset & Vine and was *the* hangout capitol of Hollywood. It stocked the most complete selection of records anywhere and far more important – had listening booths! This was a revolutionary concept. You could take a sample album into this little glass booth and play it. Without having to *buy* it!! Why not just pass out free crack?

Every kid flocked to the Topanga Plaza for one simple reason. Most of the time we were all bored. Despite what you've read about how exciting the '60s were, those of us who grew up in them spent a great deal of time looking for crap to do. When *our* children were out of school for the summer, we filled their days with karate lessons and dance classes. Back then, we just hung out, sitting around the food court, wandering aimlessly through stores (like I gave a shit about the "Raj of India's" *Pooja Accessories Sale*).

My night-life was not much better. I occasionally went to incredibly lame parties. Everyone's parents had to drive and pick you up. We were too young to drink. Too young to smoke. Too shy to really fool around. What was left was ten awkward early teens listening to music, eating snacks, drinking Cokes, and not dancing. The Amish throw better bashes.

One soiree stands out though – Bonnie Burns' birthday party. For some reason there was a photo in her living room of Steve Allen. I loved Steve Allen. Once the host of *The Tonight Show*, Allen then hosted variety programs on NBC and ABC that were far better and more cutting edge than *The Ed Sullivan Show* (as was *Lassie*). I was first introduced to Lenny Bruce on *The Steve Allen Show*. And Bob Dylan. Even Kyu Sakamoto!

There was a real sense of anarchy on his show. Allen frequently did inspired outrageous stunts. I remember one time he began his program by having a camera shoot from underneath a clear glass stage. He looked down at the camera and said, "What if a drunk suddenly staggered into your living room and saw this shot?" Wacky stuff you see on David Letterman – that all began with TV pioneers like Steve Allen (and also Ernie Kovacs).

I asked Bonnie why the picture of Allen and she said, "Because my dad is his head writer." WHAT?! HOLY SHIT!! I was in the tract house of an honest-to-goodness Rob Petrie!

Stan Burns went on to write *Get Smart* and create the series *Lancelot Link: Secret Chimp*. Picture a James Bond movie but with chimpanzees that could talk. It takes a special mind to come up with that, and a special courage to actually pitch it. Stan did and it ran for two successful years on ABC. I'm proud to say Stan Burns was my first mentor.

To this day people think I grew up in New York. They can't believe a Jewish comedy writer could come from the West San Fernando Valley. Hey, some of the funniest shows in the history of television were written right there. Not by me but *still*.

So it was the mall by day and condolence calls disguised as parties by night.

From time to time, *Where The Action Is* was filmed at the Topanga Plaza, which was quite ironic considering there was no action there *ever*. This was a daily afternoon dance show on ABC that was shot in all the "groovy" locations. If anything helped perpetuate the California Myth it was this show. They'd be at the beach, the zoo, Marineland, drag strips, Pacific Ocean Park, Knotts Berry Farm, Griffith Park stables, Pickwood Pool, Busch Gardens (a combination tropical forest/brewery – Disneyland for drunks). I say "myth" because if you didn't have a car (or worse, not know how to drive) you were shit out of luck. In all those anthems to Surf City never once do they mention getting there by city bus.

Wallichs was located in the center of the mall, across a big courtyard from Monkey Wards (where you could buy the same albums cheaper. Anyone who actually *bought* at Wallichs was an idiot). As you entered Wallichs from the courtyard you encountered a four-sided empty glass booth the size of a Beverly Hills shower. What was it for? In a couple of months I would be in it.

West San Jacinto Side Story

The summer got off to a rousing start. I spent the first two weeks in Hemet. I don't quite know why, but when old people retire in California they have this need to move out to the desert, to the middle of fucking nowhere, to lay down stakes in sweltering little dusty housing developments where the best restaurant in town is a Foster's Freeze. Throw in a couple of seedy golf courses that turn brown by February, some trailer parks, slap on names like "Sun City" or "Leisure World" and oldsters flock as if the tap water was Red Bull.

Three of my four grandparents were alive then. Nana Pearl (from my dad's side) lived in the San Fernando Valley, but Nana Lil & Grampy Sid (mom's parents) bought a house in Hemet, which is located in the San Jacinto Valley about a half-hour from hell. The town's big claim to fame is that it produced several U.S. Shuffleboard champions.

My parents flew back to New York on an "adult" trip to attend the World's Fair so my brother, Corey and I were shuttled off to Hemet. First let me say that we both loved our grandparents. Spending two weeks with Nana Lil and Grampy Sid was a joy. But

Jesus, prisoners in solitary had more to do.

Nana Lil was the classic grandmother. Great cook, energy to burn, spoiled us rotten. Grampy Sid was the most courageous man I've ever met. He lost both of his legs in World War I and wore artificial limbs for over sixty years. In fact, he was the last WWI vet still on artificial legs by the late 80s. Never once did I hear him complain or feel sorry for himself. Other than drive and maybe ski, there wasn't anything he didn't do.

Still, this was two weeks of actually living the *Napoleon Dynamite* movie.

Nana Lil saw on a flyer that there was going to be a dance at the nearby San Jacinto High and suggested I go. This did not seem a great idea to me. But Nana said, "So how you going to make friends?" "I *have* friends," I protested. "Who?" "The Gazins, Nathan and Yetta." "They're 90!" I agreed to go to the dance. Lucky Corey was too young and got to stay home with them and watch Lawrence Welk and his Champagne Music Makers on ABC perform hits from the '30s.

So on the appointed night, Nana Lil dropped me off at the school and roared away. I stepped into the gym. Adhering to the universal dance party dress code I was nattily attired in jacket and tie. Uh... no one else got the memo.

Everyone else was Hispanic, dressed in t-shirts, shorts, slutty blouses, hot pants. Many were armed. This was *West Side Story* except these weren't gay guys doing pirouettes. They had knives and cigarettes. I looked like Little Lord Fauntleroy. Thanks, Nana. But as I sat in the corner cowering for three hours, I realized this is pretty much the way I feel at *all* school social situations. The only difference here is the weapons. This was a problem if I had even a scintilla of a hope that one day I'd become "popular."

I pondered this dilemma for the rest of the week while playing canasta with the Gazins.

(Flash-forward to today and two groups still inhabit Hemet: septuagenarians and violent Mexican street gangs.)

At least I had my transistor radio. I could pick up KFXM from San Bernardino. I was sitting at the kitchen table one day, counting floor tiles and listening to the radio. Nana Lil was preparing her nightly corned beef. San Bernardino was in the throes of a crisis at that moment—a serial rapist was terrorizing the community. The station ran a public service announcement: *"Help KFXM find the hooded rapist."* Nana Lil shook her head and said, "Such a contest!"

My other grandmother, Nana Pearl, surprised me later that summer by saying, "Fuck!" You don't expect to hear your dear sweet old world, refined grandmother scream, "FUCK!!!" And at Disneyland no less.

The family made a sojourn to the Magic Kingdom and took Nana Pearl with us. At the time she was probably in her mid-60s. No one knew the ages of their Jewish grandparents back then. They all came over from Europe or Russia and no one arrived with accurate documentation. If Cher had entered the country via Ellis Island she'd claim to be 36 today.

But Nana Pearl was a kick. Always full of life. Your basic strudel-baking furniture-cleaning grandmother but game for anything… except…

Thrill rides.

So at Disneyland she was not interested in any roller coasters. We found ourselves at the Matterhorn bobsleds and of course Corey and I wanted to go. My father suggested Nana Pearl join us. He told her it was just a nice lazy boat ride. Dad has a mischievous streak in him. Either that or he was getting back at her for grounding him one weekend in 1939. Anyway, Nana Pearl agrees to go.

I'm in the back of the bobsled and Nana Pearl is in my lap. The sled slowly ascends up the center of the mountain. About halfway up she figures it out. That is when, for the first time ever, my grandmother dropped the F-bomb.

The bobsled begins hurtling down the mountain and all the while she is yelling, "I'm going to KILL him! If I ever get off of this damn thing I'm going to fucking KILL Clifford!" I didn't help matters by laughing hysterically.

I think she chased him through three Lands.

My favorite Disneyland ride at the time wasn't a ride at all. It was the Monsanto House of the Future. You just walked through this ultra modern house made entirely of plastic. A plastic house might sound ridiculous but when they finally closed the exhibit in 1967 and tried to demolish it, the wrecking ball just bounced right off of it. The one day demolition took two weeks.

Among the House of the Future's visionary features – an oven that cooked food within seconds not hours, a TV that hung like a framed picture on the wall, telephones that allowed you to *see* the other party, and the most unbelievable wonder of all – a toothbrush that was electric! You would just push a button and the bristles rotated all by themselves! I'm sorry, this was *beyond* science fiction.

Like all kids, and probably adults too in 1964, we thought that by the year 2000 we'd all be living like the Jetsons. We'd all be flying around in space ships that folded into briefcases and even brushing our teeth without having to move our hands up and down.

I Did It Amway

Fortunately, we were back home from Hemet in time for Independence Day. They still had 4th of July parades in Woodland Hills. Not exactly lavish affairs—a few Jaycee Booster Clubs, school marching bands (playing nothing but "Stars & Stripes Forever" and "Itsy Bitsy Teeny Weenie Yellow Polka Dot Bikini"), anyone who owned a horse, ice cream trucks, local dignitaries ("Hey, there's Mr. Neider from Neider's Auto Body!"), some elementary school classes, local politicians ("We have a councilman?"), and majorettes from as far away as Reseda. The twirling batons proved to be more dangerous to crowds than today's maple bats.

But for me the REAL reason to stake out my spot on Ventura Blvd at Shoup Avenue was that the grand marshal was always Buster Keaton. Buster was probably 150 by then but still, there he was. Mostly forgotten today but Buster Keaton was a comic genius in the era of silent films and early talkies. His flair for physical comedy was so inspired that even today I don't think there's a single comic who can remotely touch him. If I couldn't still see George Washington in person at least there was Buster Keaton.

I miss those parades. If you still have one where you live, go. Wave a flag. Cheer. Just duck when the baton twirlers go by.

After surviving Hemet, I got my first job. This was difficult since California labor laws required you be at least sixteen and I was still two years shy. But that didn't bother Amway.

Amway is a company that makes cleaning products sold door-to-door. It's not like you applied for a job, went through a lengthy vetting process, and were hired. You just bought the sales kit for $20 and shazam! You were a proud member of the Amway family.

My friend Mark turned me on to this golden opportunity. Mark also turned me on to *Playboy* magazine and those magnificent "Girls from Latvia" so he certainly had street cred. We went to a sales pitch where this huckster demonstrated how everyone could make six-figure incomes. Just by selling cans of spray-on shoe polish! He even had a graph (which looked suspiciously like a pyramid now that I think about it) that proved it!

So every morning I trudged off to nearby neighborhoods with my little plastic case of samples and order forms. The sales pitch was this: After the customer allows you to enter their home, conduct a series of amazing demonstrations. Spray one of their shoes. Grind dirt into their carpet and show how Amway's magic spot remover cleans it up in a jiffy. Foolproof! The truth is the products were actually excellent. They really did what they promised.

But it turns out people didn't just let a 14-year-old stranger into their homes. Who knew? Out of a hundred houses, my success rate was probably one.

And it turns out those weren't the best houses. Usually the fair maidens that invited me in were drunks in tattered nightgowns that would let Nazi Youth in if it would break up the day. Often these homes were rundown, had big gleaming motorboats in the driveway and no furniture, or a brand new color TV/Hi-fi console and orange crates.

I think for the entire summer I made $25.00. Then Amway billed me $20.00 for the plastic case and $1.75 for the handout brochures. After ignoring four of these rather rude invoices, I received a no-nonsense letter from an attorney threatening to sue me and seize all of my assets (which at the time meant baseball cards and a thousand bad Connie Francis 45's). I dashed them off a reply reminding them I was 14. They were employing a minor. The threats ceased.

The plastic case broke in September.

You Never Forget Your First Whore

I got my first moving violation that same month. Apparently I did not bring my bicycle to a complete stop at a stop sign. Usually cops will write you a citation and have you report to the Juvenile Court where an officer will give you a safety comic book.

I was told to report to Van Nuys Municipal Court. Gulp! My father had to give up a half day of work to drive me there. This was a *real* court, with a judge and bailiff, and public defenders.

The other defendants were all drug dealers, wife beaters, gang members. I was scared shitless. I would have pissed on myself if one of the other gentlemen hadn't been fined $200 for doing that same thing in a Piggly Wiggly market.

This judge was throwing the book at everybody. $200 here, two nights in jail there. No one was spared. I had visions of being led off in handcuffs and reduced to selling Amway products to inmates to make my bail.

Three young women were summoned to stand before the court. They were all dressed in halter tops and hot pants, one had a big ratty fur wrapped around her neck. Probably coyote. They were being charged with illegal solicitation.

Ohmygod! They were PROSTITUTES! Real live whores!! I was actually in a room with women who had sex. Forget that it was for money; just the fact that they were *doing it* was unbelievable to me. In my incredibly naïve, bordering-on-retarded, mind I believed that no girl *wanted* sex. Only boys did. And once married, girls begrudgingly did it, but only to start a family, or at the very least, to shut him up. I never for a moment thought they might *enjoy* it too. I should've been on trial for ignorance.

I went from terrified to aroused. I could not take my eyes off these ladies of the evening. I wondered if I could cash in my Bar Mitzvah Saving Bonds to buy an hour with one of them. Imagine! Having sex with a girl who didn't cry afterwards!

I was jolted back into grim reality when the bailiff called my name. It's amazing what a buzz kill pending incarceration is. I approached the bench, my father by my side for support.

"Not stopping at a stop sign? This is *serious*!" Really? I was soooo dead.

The judge glared at my father. "Mr. Levine, isn't your son a little young to be driving an automobile?" "Uh, it wasn't a car, your honor, it was a bicycle." "What?" barked the judge, "Aw, Christ! Case dismissed!"

You'd think I'd learn my lesson. But I was so girl crazy I went through every stop sign I saw just *hoping* to get caught.

Woodland Hills Weed

That mystery glass booth at Wallichs remained empty until late July. And then an odd control panel appeared inside. Ominous with a big circular green fluorescent screen surrounded by blinking pen lights and toggle switches. Was Bond-supervillain Dr. No going to move his world domination operation to a shopping mall and fire his nuclear missiles from a Woodland Hills store window?

What the hell was this thing?

Two turntables and a microphone arrived.

Holy shit! It was a radio station studio! And not just *any* station. KFWB!

Back in the '60s radio played a big part in the life of a teenager. As unfathomable as it may seem, kids could not access music through their phones back then. They had to rely on AM radio. A fierce loyalty developed between the listener and station. Most cities had two competing rockers and you were aligned with one or the other. I was a KFWB man over KRLA. Why? I have no idea. They were both exactly the same.

That station loyalty and identification extended to the disc jockeys.

A local survey revealed that L.A. teenagers trusted disc jockeys more than their parents, teachers, policemen, even their religious leaders. (I still haven't decided whether that's admirable or really sad.)

But one of my favorites was KFWB's Gene Weed. Picture David Caruso but younger, not craggy, not a weasel.

Gene would now be doing his show every Saturday afternoon from Wallichs. There *is* a God!

This would be a two-man operation. The engineer manning the turntables and Gene across from him at the mike. Outside, pimple faced kids pressed their faces against the glass like canned hams. Mine included.

Most would watch for ten minutes and then move on to the similar, and more lively, monkey cages. Not me. My schmooshed face never left its spot. I knew I had to get in there. Somehow.

Fate smiled when Gene showed up one day with a cold. I raced down to Kaplan's mediocre Deli and returned with a Styrofoam cup of their horrible chicken soup. A gofer had been born.

From that Saturday on, I stood in the corner, watching in awe as he introduced records and made golf reservations over the phone. This was the life for me, I thought. At 14, I had found my calling. Forget that at eight I had also found my calling as a baseball announcer, and at six I saw myself driving a steam shovel.

One week the all-night man, Larry McCormick filled in. Larry was the first African-American to crossover from R & B radio to a Top 40 mainstream station.

He was also the first person to tell me *I'm an idiot if I go into radio.* I was stunned. He cautioned that disc jockeys had limited futures and the industry itself was just a cut above traveling medicine shows. I would come to learn years later that he was absolutely right. But at the time I was mystified. (Larry McCormick went on to break the color barrier in local TV news and became the first African-American anchor. And Gene Weed fled radio to become a top TV director.)

But in the late summer of 1964, I couldn't think of a better way of spending six or seven decades than by playing "My Boy Lollipop."

Larry Lujack, a top rated jock in Chicago for much of the '60s and '70s was often asked, "What do you say to a kid who wants to be a disc jockey when he grows up?" and Larry would say, "You can't do both."

Hard Day's Nukes

I've always been fascinated by the National Conventions. I am hardly what you'd call a wonk but (a) these political bacchanals were great theater, and (b) there was nothing else on; even ABC pre-empted programming.

At one time there was great drama at these back-slap-fests. You didn't know who the presidential candidates were going to be until *after* the conventions, not three months before. Today the only suspense is, can you stay awake? But back then it was rollicking good fun – thousands of goofballs in straw hats and bolo ties waving campaign signs and hoping to get the West Virginia delegates into the sack.

Four years later it would not be as amusing, but that's getting ahead of myself.

Each of the three major networks provided their own coverage. Most households had a decided preference. We were a CBS family. Uncle Walter Cronkite conveyed trust, reassurance, and objectivity. There was no CBS News "with an attitude," no "Cronkite Factor." Just a middle-aged, rumpled reporter who looked more like your family doctor than Chad who cleans your pool.

NBC countered with the equally credible "Huntley-Brinkley Report." Chet Huntley was the stern father with the voice of God. You always expected him to take you out to the back of the woodshed if you talked during his newscast. David Brinkley was the nerd who made good. Together they developed a large following. No one watched ABC's coverage. When the crown jewel of your primetime schedule is *The Patty Duke Show*, it's hard to take the news division seriously.

The Democratic Convention was in Atlantic City. Senator Robert Kennedy introduced a short film on his late brother and received a 22-minute standing ovation. Hubert Humphrey was named the Vice President candidate and got the kind of delirious reception normally reserved for amateur comics on open mic night.

I missed LBJ's nomination acceptance speech. That night I was in the Corbin Theater watching *A Hard Day's Night* starring the Beatles. A lot of history took place in the '60s while my generation was off doing something else. *A Hard Day's Night* elicited a 90-minute standing ovation, along with continuous shrieking, screaming, and swooning. The crazed girl next to me kept crying out "Paul! Paul! Paul!!" "That's a screen!" I yelled, finally. "He can't hear you!"

The Beatles *were* live in Los Angeles on August 23rd. I did not attend the concert. Tickets were expensive ($4.00 apiece!), impossible to get, and Mom wasn't too keen on driving by the Hollywood Bowl and picking me up out front.

The Republicans convened in the aptly named Cow Palace in San Francisco, choosing Barry *"what's the point of having nukes if you don't use 'em?"* Goldwater as their nominee and right-wing Bill Miller as his running mate. (Ironically, Miller's daughter is Stephanie Miller, the left-wing talk show host. On the scale of rebellious children, that ranks above the minister's daughter who becomes a whore.)

Highlight of that convention was when NBC reporter, John

Chancellor was ejected from the main floor. Wearing bulky headphones and an aerial sticking out of the top of his head, he was led away by security thugs on national television. He signed off by saying: "This is John Chancellor, somewhere in custody." Live television was so much more fun when they still had no idea what they were doing yet.

LBJ and Gypsy Boots

The fall of '64 was somewhat of a blur. I reluctantly accepted an invitation to join Parkman's honor society, "the Vanguards" thereby cementing my status as the un-hippest kid in school. George Putnam announced, "Herbert Hoover is DEAD!!!!" Two American destroyers engaged three North Vietnamese torpedo boats in the Gulf of Tonkin. There was a question about it on our weekly quiz. I got it wrong. It didn't seem important at the time. It was only just the start of the Vietnam War. And decades later we would learn it was just a complete fabrication, dreamed up by the administration to acquire war powers. When people say "Remember Pearl Harbor" it's somewhat easier to do since the Japanese attack on Pearl Harbor actually *existed*.

I was marking time. Only one more semester until high school and full adulthood. My taste in women was beginning to change, I noticed. I developed a preference for the more *exotic* type. My crush *du jour* was Jackie Sharf – the perfect blend of Marcia Brady and biker chick. Alas, she had a boyfriend... who was in high school! That was the infuriating trend. All the foxy seniors (*foxy* being the preferred word back then) in junior high went out with high schoolers and all the foxy seniors in high school only dated college boys. You could never date a girl in your own grade. Women always seemed to go for the *older guys*. They went out with high school boys because they had cars, and then in later years they went out with guys as old as their fathers because they *bought* them cars.

Johnson trounced Goldwater in November. But he really won on September 7th. That's when, on *David & Bathsheba* (NBC's Monday Night Movie) his campaign aired one thirty-second commercial. An idyllic little girl is in an idyllic little meadow picking daisies and counting the idyllic pedals. When she reaches "nine" an ominous movie-trailer voice launches into a missile countdown. The cherub looks to the sky, the camera zooms in until her black pupil is all we can see. There's a flash and a mushroom cloud from a nuclear explosion. LBJ then drawls: "*These are the stakes! To make a world in which all of God's children can live, or to go into the dark. We must either love each other, or we must die.*" Graciously allowing the audience a second to shit in their pants, another announcer says, "*Vote for President Johnson on November 3. The stakes are too high for you to stay home.*"

150,000,000 Americans must've watched *David & Bathsheba* because the ad ran just that once yet everyone says they saw it. Everyone but me. I was watching *I've Got A Secret* on CBS. I had a crush on panelist, Bess Meyerson.

Thanksgiving finally arrived and with it the cheese-rich Santa Claus Lane Parade down Hollywood Blvd. Unlike Macy's with giant balloons and impressive marching bands, we had Hollywood B-actors, second bananas, local fringe celebrities riding in cars with their names hand-painted on the sides, and a few 100-year-old guys from an American Legion Post blowing their livers out through trombones. The big finale was the arrival of Santa Claus; usually on a float that looked like a Cub Scout project gone horribly wrong.

I never actually *attended* the parade. My parents were not about to wade through a million people so I could see talk show guest Oscar Levant either waving to the crowd or having another seizure. If we couldn't walk to it (like the 4th of July parade) my folks weren't interested. But I didn't care. It was a TV event anyway.

Bill Welsh on Channel 11 would interview all the "stars" as they passed. How do you ask Gypsy Boots what his upcoming project was with a straight face? Gypsy Boots was a local health nut who was part Grizzly Adams/part Bozo the Clown. His upcoming *project*??? Appear in *next* year's parade. Back in the '50s, Natalie Wood or Bing Crosby would be the grand marshal. Now it was Iron Eyes Cody.

After the Christmas rush, KFWB decided to discontinue broadcasting from the Topanga Plaza. I was quite bummed out. But on the scale of losses from *one-to-Ann*, I only rated KFWB's bailing a five. 1965 was right around the corner. A new school. New experiences. So much to look forward to.

PART TWO

Kind of a Drag

Watched Lyndon Johnson's Inaugural Address in history class. Not the "Ask Not What..." inspirational address we received from Kennedy. *Camelot* had been replaced by *Hemet*. Four years ago we cheered. Today we held our collective breath.

Graduation Day finally arrived at the end of January. For some unfathomable reason, I agreed to give one of the commencement speeches. The topic I was assigned was "the Joy of Service." Not a lot of soup kitchens in Woodland Hills so I decided to focus on the Peace Corps. (a holdover from the Kennedy era). I waxed on and on about its virtues – helping the less fortunate of the world, spreading democracy, bridging cultures. By the end I almost wanted to join myself. (Thirty years later my writing partner David Isaacs and I would write the Tom Hanks/John Candy movie *Volunteers* about the Peace Corps. Sargent Shriver, the program's first director read a copy of our screenplay and said, "It was like spitting on the flag.") Maybe I should have given the speech on something I knew: "The Joy of Masturbation."

Graduation was Friday. The following Monday, February 1st, I began high school. And my dad began a new job. He moved over from KRKD to the much more successful, prestigious, and listened-to KABC. It pays to dress in drag and sing in public.

Okay, that's not the *only* reason Dad got the job… but it helped.

Backstory: There was an organization in the LA broadcast community called "The Miline Club." Many of the big radio and agency execs belonged. It was essentially a men's club. They would have monthly luncheons and other activities. It was a chance to talk shop and drink heavily during the day (like they needed an excuse). Their one big event was a gala Broadway musical parody, staged one time a year during the Christmas season in the same humungous ballroom that hosts the Golden Globes. It was a lavish affair, complete with costumes, props, an orchestra, choreographer, and that staple of the Great White Way—a stripper. Members would play all the parts, even the women. Tickets were in hot demand. Where else were you going to see the president of a major advertising agency or general manager of a top radio station prancing around a stage dressed as Maria from *The Sound of Music*? These pillars of industry were GREAT sports.

As were their wives. I remember Mom once saying to Dad, "Shave your legs this year."

It should be noted that these parodies were filthy. Just one unconscionable, inappropriate, jaw-dropping, body part joke after another. If there were sexual harassment suits back then, each one of these men would be sent away for a thousand years. But it was all in good fun, a way to raise some money (the "Joy of Service"), and a great opportunity to network. Through the Miline Club, Dad made some terrific contacts and when the account executive position opened at KABC he was on their radar. The lesson I chose to take from this was that networking was important, not an easy concept to embrace for one who was basically shy and had no idea how to accessorize.

Nuns, Nazis, and Sex Education

So I was finally at Taft. Three years later I couldn't wait to get out, but *still*. As high schools go, this was a lovely new facility. More like an industrial park than a school, Taft was a series of modern two-story buildings. How perfect that it was featured in *The Brady Bunch Movie*.

There was not a lot of diversity in the Taft High student body. Enrollment was 2,000. 1,999 of us were white. Our one African-American was a football star. Everyone was *overly* accepting of him. The Civil Rights marches and incidents were beginning to make an impression (and he scored a lot of touchdowns). Like I said, we were pretty far removed from where the black population lived. Personally, I don't believe the twenty-minutes I spent driving lost in their community was sufficient to really understand their predicament and culture. But it was still twenty more minutes than most of my classmates had ever experienced.

I can't say there was the same school tolerance for gays, however. Especially compared to today. There were no Gay Rights clubs at Taft. So I don't really know how many gays there were because they stayed in the closet. Puberty is a time of massive insecurity, when kids feel inadequate about themselves for so many reasons, and often try to compensate by diminishing others. Gays were an easy target. When you really wanted to put someone down you called him *a homo, a queer, a fag*, as if he were some lower species. And those were fightin' words. The accused would be compelled to defend his honor and manhood. Unless it was me. I could care less what those mouth-breathers called me.

I have to say though, that as our generation matured we really became more open-minded about homosexuality, more so than any generation previously. But that was little comfort to those who were forced to keep their sexual preference to themselves at "liberal" Taft High in 1965.

I knew only one kid who was obviously gay. Randy Melman. He was a classmate in the 7th Grade, my age, and even though it perpetuates every cliché and stereotype, he played the *Judy Garland at Carnegie Hall* album constantly. But I really liked him. He had a sense of humor. We hated the same people. And he was pretty much the only "guy" I felt comfortable sharing my feelings with. Randy helped me get through the tragic Ann crisis. Although I'm not gay myself, I always felt a bond with him. I too thought of myself as an outsider and a weird kid. Is *Judy Garland at Carnegie Hall* any worse than announcing little league games into a tape recorder and reading beer commercials between innings? Randy transferred to a private school in the 8th Grade, one that was more welcoming and had no football program.

Meanwhile, at Taft, the first day was class registration. I was used to just being given my schedule. No. Not in *high* school. Here you ran for classes. Everyone scrambled around the gym trying to cobble together a schedule. (A Filenes's Basement sale, except you flung people to the ground to get Algebra II not a sweater.) Everything closed fast. By the end of the day I wound up three classes short and had somehow signed up for Home Economics. (No wonder they called me *homo*.)

Day two, a counselor helped straighten things out. He was also the basketball coach and (noticing I was 6' 2" and could walk), invited me to take his basketball class instead of general P.E. I thought, great, I hate P.E. Instead of insufferable calisthenics, I'd be shooting hoops all day.

Uh, wrong.

It was essentially a conditioning class. All we did was run. Mile after vomit inducing mile. Meanwhile, the general P.E. classes played basketball.

I shared a school locker with my reunited best friend, Gary McMahon. He was quite excited, having just returned from a high school Job Fair. Remember, this was a time when we all really *believed* we could be anything we wanted to be. The lavish medical, legal, and business industry displays were crowded with students. Gary was the lone person at the Mortuary Science booth. But it was worth it for the handful of post cards he picked up from The National Casket Company, showing off their spiffiest maple model. For years Gary would anonymously send them to teachers, prom kings, and star athletes with the caption "Wish You Were Here." Revenge of the really lame Nerds.

My parents took me to see *The Sound Of Music* at the Carthay Center Theatre for my Valentine's Day birthday. Why they thought a 15 year-old boy would be remotely interested in that, I do not know. When did I ever show an interest in nuns, Nazis, or production numbers? Plus, whenever Julie Andrews was on the screen, all I could picture was my father.

But going to the Carthay Center was a big deal. Reserved seats. Intermission. You got dressed up. The film would win the Best Picture Oscar, but I sure would have preferred seeing *Cat Ballou* for the third time at the Corbin on Ventura. No one pulled off sex kitten/political activist/light comedy better than Jane Fonda.

I had carved out a lot of extra study time because this was *high* school and the workload would undoubtedly increase exponentially. For the first two weeks I studied every waking hour. By week three, when I was so far ahead it was ridiculous, I realized that the amount of homework was no greater than last year's. I found myself at a crossroads. I could continue to study this diligently and probably get straight A's or return to my normal study habits and get B's but never miss *The Lloyd Thaxton Show*. Guess which path I took.

First year classes tended to be generic. "Science" instead of "Chemistry" or "Biology." "English" instead of "British Literature" or "Shakespeare." These courses were a challenge – to stay awake during.

The contrast between junior and senior high was not nearly as great as I had thought. All the girls had breasts instead of just some and there was no "Nutrition," but otherwise – pretty much same-old, same-old. On one hand, I was relieved. High school had always seemed so daunting. On the other, after all the build-up and anticipation, *this* was the big deal? I wondered if I'd feel the same way about sex (if, and when I ever had it).

Among my classes that first semester was Health. "Aunt Bea" from *The Andy Griffith Show* taught us the correct way to brush our teeth, clean our ears, and treat vaginal discharge. Under the guise of sex education we were shown a steady parade of *informational films* designed to scare the shit out of us. They were always these little black-and-white dramas. "Bobby" and "Linda" disobeying their wise parents and being *promiscuous*.

Part one, Linda got pregnant. Part two, they both got gonorrhea. Part three Linda became a whore. The girls in class seemed horribly shaken by all this. The boys just wanted to see Linda naked.

There were also cautionary drug docudramas on marijuana and drug use. These always featured "Jimmy." (Bobby was in an insane asylum by then with syphilis.) Jimmy was a good kid but weak willed. He bumps into an old friend (who looks like Satan) and is invited to a party. He disobeys his wise parents and goes, even though it's a school night. Everyone is smoking marijuana and listening to that *jungle music*. At the risk of being called a "square," Jimmy takes a puff. Part two is a week later. Jimmy is now a drug addict, shooting up, stealing to maintain his habit, hanging out with girls who wear slacks. Part three, he's arrested and must go through withdrawal. We see him in agony, thrashing around in his cell, screaming for what we're told will be 48 straight hours.

I must confess, at the time, the drug films did sell me somewhat. Not that I assumed one toke would turn Jimmy into Lenny Bruce, but it did give me pause. And this was still the period where a clear line existed between good kids (like me and my friends) and *bad* kids (drug users/shop majors). Less than a year later that distinction would be completely blurred, but in 1965 my drugs of choice were unattainable girls, baseball, and radio.

Will Sitcoms Make You Go Blind?

In March, President Johnson unveiled an ambitious urban renewal bill he called "The Great Society." I suppose this sweeping program benefited many people. It had no effect on my life whatsoever. I'm surprised I even remember it.

In my insular cocoon, I was getting $5.00 a week allowance. Out of that largesse I bought records, movie passes, Clearasil, junk food, Stridex Medicated Pads, surf magazines – y'know, the *essentials*. In the mid '60s *my g-g-g-g-generation* would spend $11 billion on such essentials. By 1970 we would spend $70 billion. I guess they started figuring in drugs.

It was a banner year for television. *My Mother The Car* premiered. (Has there ever been a more terrifying Oedipal concept for a teenage boy than his mother being his car? Short of *My Mother The Dick*, I can't think of anything worse.) More shows were being shown in color. We didn't have a color TV, but I knew more people who did so *that* was exciting.

Sitcoms for the most part were lame. *Petticoat Junction* (which opens with the three starring girls bathing in the town's water supply— but I had a crush on the three girls), *The Patty Duke Show* (she played identical cousins Patty & Cathy and wasn't funny as either. But I had a crush on her… or them), *The Donna Reed Show* (I had a crush on Shelley Fabares), *Bewitched* (I had a crush on Elizabeth Montgomery), *Mr. Ed* (I had a crush on Connie Hines), *Camp Runamuck* (I had a crush on Maureen McCormick), and *Gidget* (I had a *major* crush on Sally Field). Most people watched sitcoms to laugh. I watched them to masturbate.

Teenage characters in '60s comedies were all written by 50 year-old men. We were all portrayed as fun-loving *kooks* who got into "jams" and were usually bailed out by our (coincidentally) 50 year-old fathers. Boys were all oversexed, which meant we wanted to "go steady" before the girls were ready. Girls were oversexed too and were willing to "put out" for the right *dreamy* boy… and by "put out" I mean accept a double-date for miniature golf. It was a fairy world. Just once I wanted to see Gidget pass out not because Moondoggie invited her to the prom, but because she had severe menstrual cramps.

April brought the Spring break.

In Montgomery, Alabama, four Ku Klux Klan members kill a freedom marcher. Their Grand Imperial Wizard announces the formation of a youth chapter, which he says will be like "*the Boy Scouts.*" Civil Rights marches are appearing more and more on the news. And I'm starting to watch the news more and more. I don't know whether it's because I'm maturing at 15 or just becoming aware that the world is a scary place and getting scarier. Maybe I better pay attention.

But for now, I go to the Teenage Fair.

The Hollywood Palladium was an art deco theater built in the '40s in Hollywood to stage big band concerts. In the '60s it was the spring break home of the Teenage Fair. The Palladium inside and outside was filled with exhibits and booths. Guitars on display, decals, flyers, motorcycles, dance contests, electronic equipment, cosmetics, surfing demonstrations, radio remotes, record racks, and live concerts. Meanwhile, on the side of the building there was a large billboard showcasing Nana Lil's favorite—Lawrence Welk and his Champagne Music Makers, complete with bubbles that were supposed to ascend from a champagne flute but instead appeared to come from his nose.

I wanted to bring a date but the two-hour bus ride each way was a problem for those princesses.

I'm guessing the fair was a lot more happening at 10:00 on Friday and Saturday nights. But at noon on a Tuesday it was pretty dead. In ten minutes I was already bored. So I meandered past the drug paraphernalia exhibit and adjacent Army recruiting booth (yes, I recognized the irony even back then) to see which *superstar* was performing in the main room. It was a couple and they were god-awful. No wonder they were booked for the lunch hour. She was this scrawny Goth chick and he was this middle-aged goomba with a huge schnoz, a Beatle haircut, and a fur vest. Luigi Flintstone & Morticia. She at least could sing. He sounded like an ambulance siren. There were maybe eight of us watching this pathetic display, convinced that these were the two biggest losers on the planet. On the other hand, I can say I discovered Sonny & Cher.

Tina Delgado is Alive! Alive!

KHJ was a local radio station that no one ever listened to. They changed formats more than Elizabeth Taylor changed husbands. As 1965 began they switched again. All ice skating music this time? No. Top 40 (even though they had already failed twice with that format). A guy who successfully programmed stations in cosmopolitan Fresno and Stockton was hired to create it. His competing program director in Fresno, recently released from a Hong Kong jail, was tabbed to be the program director. Together Bill Drake and Ron Jacobs would revolutionize the entire radio industry. In three months KHJ "Boss Radio" was number one in Los Angeles, toppling stalwarts KFWB and KRLA, and within a year there was a "Boss Radio" clone in every market in the country. No one stopped to ask, "What the fuck does *Boss* even mean?" They just copied the formatics and their ratings skyrocketed.

From the moment I heard it, I was hooked. This was a high energy, streamlined bullet train. Their slogan was "More Music" but it could have been the more catchy "Adrenaline till you have a grand mal seizure." For the next four years I listened to KHJ every waking moment I wasn't listening to Vin Scully and the Dodgers. The disc jockeys ("Boss Jocks") became my constant companions. Sort of like "imaginary friends" who took song requests. My favorites were Robert W. Morgan in the morning with his biting wit and insane madman "the Real Don Steele" in the afternoon. Steele was this larger-than-life, fast-talking hipster who completely captivated Southern California teenagers. For no reason whatsoever he would scream out, *"Tina Delgado is alive! Alive!"* We boomers loved rallying cries, even if they made no sense.

(Moviegoers know the Real Don Steele as the guy who got electrocuted in *Eating Raoul* and impaled in *Death Race 2000*. Years later I worked with him and one of my most cherished memories was seeing him get so drunk one night he fell off our living room couch.)

KHJ tapped into the psyche of my generation. I'll leave the socio and psychoanalysis to the historians, but the bottom line is we all just wanted to party. And Boss Radio was one continuous party, which held even greater significance to those of us who never got invited to parties.

She's So Fine

I missed Ann's failed pilot. It was called *Alec Tate* and even though it didn't get picked up to series, the network still aired it in the summer along with their other unsold projects. The industry nickname for this practice was *Failure Theater*. But prior to *Alec Tate*, I never missed an Ann Jillian TV appearance. I skipped High Holiday services to see her on *Hazel*. And here's the thing: I knew *Alec Tate* was going to be on. I *chose* not to watch it.

The spell had been broken.

Thank you, Bev Fine.

Bev Fine wasn't just another crush. This was actual obsession bordering on mental illness. In other words – teenage love. It's hard to say just why Bev Fine rose above the many other potential heartthrobs but she did. Sorry gals (not that you cared).

Bev had the classic California Girl look – blond, beautiful, and out-of-my-league, but she was also a *member of the tribe*. Finally! A Jewish Gidget!

Except she didn't surf. Who are we kidding? None of the girls did. They'd lie on towels on the beach, slather Coppertone tanning lotion on their already bronze bodies (its big selling point: *Nothing* to block the sun!!), and wrestle over which surfer boy to lose their virginity to.

Bev was also approachable. Unlike Dana (who still lurked in the hallways, adding six months of therapy with every sighting), Bev was a sweetheart. You could talk to her and genuinely get the feeling she wouldn't be mortified if her friends saw. Not that I wasn't still completely terrified that at any moment I would slip and say something she'd find offensive and never want to speak to me again, but I felt comfortable (brave) enough to pursue an actual friendship. If they wouldn't agree to sex, at least they'd say hello to you in the hash line, and isn't that, y'know, almost as good?

I didn't become her boyfriend. But I did become her agent.

Bev wanted to be an actress. What was it with me and actresses? (I have since, in my adult years, discovered this empirical truth: Never date actresses. 98% of them never make it, become bitter, and you pay for it, or worse—they *do* make it and leave you for George Clooney.) But as kids we were just role-playing. I offered to be her "agent." It became a running bit between us. We'd pass in the hall and I'd say, "I'm expecting a call from Otto Preminger. Hang in there. I might have something big for you."

Looking back, I should have told her how I really felt about her. I should have realized just by her personality that Bev wouldn't react the way Dana did. But I was still waaaaay too insecure. My lame attempt to build self-esteem was to buy a set of *Ted Williams* bar bells from Sears. What was I thinking? Ted Williams wasn't even a body builder. He was a baseball player. He was known as the "Splendid Splinter." *That's* who I wanted to bulk up and emulate? A guy who looked like a stick? For weeks I would "pump iron" in my bedroom, not knowing how to do any of it of course. (The back problems I have today probably stem from those afternoon workout sessions.)

Finally it warmed up and I was able to wear a short-sleeve shirt. Bev was sure to swoon now. I stood at the mirror admiring the *new me* and flexed my new bicep. But what I saw was a little anthill on an otherwise scrawny arm. That was the end of Ted Williams and short-sleeve shirts.

Besides, I tried to convince myself that I couldn't really take Bev out on a date anyway. I couldn't drive yet. *Next* year. I'll make my big play then. For now, I can just enjoy our friendship and wait for her call-back from Otto.

Watts Happening

I hadn't had a reality check since the Kennedy assassination. Following those four days of inescapable grief, life pretty much carried on. It's hard to say the tenor of the country changed when in 1965 there was not one but three new Elvis movies released... with titles like *Girl Happy, Tickle Me*, and *Harum Scarum*.

But a water skiing trip and a riot would change my worldview.

One weekend in July, our neighbors, the Urangas, invited us to go water skiing with them. They had the boat. So off the shores of Carlsbad I failed to learn how to water-ski. That night we all went to a local pizza joint and Mrs. Uranga started talking about her brother who had just returned from a tour of duty in Vietnam. He reported that it was a complete mess over there. Utter chaos. We had no business being there and there was no way to win because we had no idea *who* the enemy was or how to fight them. This was in stark contrast to what our government was saying. According to them, we were clearly winning what was a vital mission. As self-appointed guardians of the world, it was up to us to preserve freedom in the world. And if the Commies were allowed to conquer Vietnam then Cambodia, Laos, and Catalina would surely fall next. It was the Domino Theory. Stop them now or in ten years we would all be eating borscht.

It was hard to believe our government would misrepresent this skirmish. We *trusted* our government. It was their sworn duty to be honest with us, right? So for the moment I thought this returning soldier (or "advisor" as they were called then) was just disgruntled because he was passed over for General or something. But there was something so unsettling about his warning that it always stayed with me.

And just how naïve a country were we at that time? A popular television show was *The Man From U.N.C.L.E* – a James Bond rip-off. The United Nations' General Services Division was deluged with letters and telephone calls from people wanting to actually join the fictitious U.N.C.L.E.

That was July. In August, a California Highway Patrolman stopped an inebriated black man in Watts. (Note: Back then African-Americans preferred the term "black." It sure made James Brown's later anthem less clunky. "*Say it loud/ I'm African-American and I'm proud!*" just doesn't have the same zing to it.) When the cop tried to have the car impounded a crowd gathered and things escalated. The bottled up frustrations and oppression that had been simmering for generations finally exploded. Within 24 hours there was a full-scale riot.

For nearly a week, I watched on TV stunned and horrified as these people destroyed and looted their own neighborhood, the same neighborhood I drove through looking for *Shindig*. Storefronts were set on fire. Windows were smashed. The National Guard was sent in. It was insane. You'd see two kids hauling a couch down the street as bricks and rocks flew and fistfights raged on in the background. Not a movie, not a re-enactment. Live. *Real* reality television. In a place I'd been.

This was an utter shock to me. In my sheltered suburban life I had no real clue that there even *was* that degree of intense frustration. On those few occasions when I listened to something other than KHJ, one of my favorite stations was KGFJ. I've always loved Rhythm & Blues, and KGFJ was *the* soul station in Los Angeles. Watts, South Central, Compton – these were not ghettos; they were all just part of the "Big K Kingdom." Now they were all on fire. And KGFJ was unfairly assigned some of the blame.

Their most popular disc jockey was the Magnificent Montague. When he played a record he really liked he would yell, "Burn!" Some rioters adopted that phrase and "Burn, baby, burn!" became the unofficial rally cry. Some later thought that Montague was inciting the crowd on the radio but, in truth, he was doing just the opposite. And I know because I was listening.

On the other hand, there was Joe Pyne.

Joe Pyne was one of the first belligerent radio talk show hosts. He discovered that you could get big ratings by telling callers to "go gargle with razor blades." In the mid '60s he also had a local Saturday night television show on KTTV. He sat behind a desk while a studio audience of Cro-Magnons grunted support. On this night he waved a handgun saying every citizen should have one and be willing to use it. He was not fired for this. And the next year NBC hired him to host a daytime game show.

By Sunday the riot had run its course, leaving about $200 million in property damage. Shockingly, public opinion polls at the time showed as many people blamed the Communists for the riot as those who blamed social issues and prejudice.

For six days I remained glued to my TV. The images were inconceivable.

We're not in Surf City anymore, Dorothy.

Otherwise, the summer was spent hanging out at various places hoping I'd bump into Bev Fine. My choices:

The Topanga Plaza mall. The nearby Fallbrook Square mall (but they were an *outdoor* mall and their two anchor stores were Sears and J.C. Penney's so they catered more to the Frank Sinatra Jr. kidnappers crowd). Shakey's (holding down the fort of hellacious pizza until Chuck E. Cheese could come along), Ferrell's Ice Cream parlor (a recommended coed stalking location), and my personal favorite – Bob's Big Boy.

Founded by Bob Wian in 1936 in nearby Glendale, its signature item was the "Big Boy Hamburger." Imagine a Big Mac that actually tasted good. And Bob's trademark character was a fat cherub in checkerboard overalls and suspenders holding a double-decked hamburger. When the restaurant became a local chain in the '50s, each location featured a large statue of this tubbo (let's call him Bob) guarding the entrance. I now have one in my house. I cherish it as much as my Emmy.

Bob's Big Boy also featured carhop service and the timing couldn't have been better. The '50s had heralded in the age of the automobile. Every acne-scarred Tom, Dick, and James Dean had to have "wheels." The car culture became synonymous with Southern California. It was just like *American Graffiti*. Everybody *cruised* on Friday and Saturday nights. And you built up a hearty appetite driving up and down the same four blocks fifty times. So Bob's became the hot rod headquarters. And remained so until the early '70s gas shortage. Kids suddenly thought long and hard about cruising Van Nuys Blvd. for four hours when gasoline cost a whole *dollar* a gallon.

I also got to the beach (when I also got a ride). Zuma, Topanga, Malibu, Paradise Cove – those were "valley" beaches. We'd set out blankets on the fairly crowded sand. KHJ echoed from everyone's transistor. No one had umbrellas. Nothing to impede that rich brown tan. It's amazing we're all still alive and not blind.

Another thing the Beach Boys and Jan & Dean never warned us about in their gooey harmony-rich anthems to LA beaches – the water was *freezing*! Maybe, just maybe, at the end of a real sweltering summer the water temperature would climb to 68. Usually, it was 62 degrees or colder. But everyone went in. No one ever thought not to. Thousands of people all inching in, faces clenched, shivering, trying to convince themselves this was fun. But you never heard about *that* in those surf sounds. I guess they just couldn't find a word that rhymed with *hypothermia*.

I never bumped into Bev Fine. Not once. Turns out she spent most of her time at the Shoup pool. I never thought to look there.

The Shoup pool was a two-minute walk… from my house.

The Sunset Strip

If you were going to drive into the city from Woodland Hills it meant you were going "over the hill." Whether it be Hollywood or Westwood or even San Diego – it was "over the hill." And you only went "over the hill" if you had a real purpose. You'd think we were living in the Texas Panhandle and had to pack saddlebacks to ride into town for vittles.

But there was a new attraction that the kids were buzzing about. The Sunset Strip. In the '40s and '50s this stretch of Sunset Blvd. between Beverly Hills and Hollywood had been nightclub row. Sinatra played there. Sammy played there. Dino even had his own club. These hot spots featured dance floors and palm trees and exotic names like the Macambo, the Trocadero, Casa Manana, and Ciro's. I was never actually *in* any of these nightclubs but there were several Warner Brothers cartoons that spoofed them so I had a pretty good idea of what went on there thanks to Bugs Bunny.

Now the clubs were starting to cater to young people. Whisky A Go Go led the charge. Some say it was because of the location, others say popular singer Johnny Rivers was the big draw, but I contend it was the hot girls in mini skirts dancing in suspended cages that attracted the crowds. Rock groups would stagger down from Laurel

Canyon to perform. The Byrds, The Doors (in matching suits), The Seeds, Buffalo Springfield, Love, and even the great Captain Beefheart performed in clubs like Gazzari's, London Fog, and Pandora's Box. They weren't content to just do cover versions of popular songs or pale imitations of current styles. No sir. They delved into musical roots, experimented; challenged themselves to become artists in the truest sense of the word. Their music was new and daring and groundbreaking. God, the action those douchebags must've gotten.

The problem was these clubs couldn't serve alcohol to underage teens. And of course, they make their money off the bar. State laws prohibited anyone under 21 from even entering such establishments. Some clubs just forfeited liquor and figured the sheer volume of teen business would compensate for it. The Trip and It's Boss were two such clubs.

Other clubs were sneakier. They started serving food. So all of a sudden their establishments were considered "restaurants" and anyone could enter. Teens had to have their hands stamped, identifying them as underage, but who are we kidding? A jam packed club, strobe lighting, frenetic dancing – A Doberman Pinscher could buy a bottle of Schlitz and no one would notice.

My 17-year-old cousin Craig was visiting from Louisville that summer. So for two weeks I had a chauffer. One night we ventured "over the hill" and cruised down the Sunset Strip. We must've looked like the Beverly Hillbillies gawking at all the activity. We were lucky and found a parking space only a mile up the hill from the strip and we headed down to "check out the scene." Who's hipper than a 15-year-old who still draws comics and a kid from Kentucky?

People were just hanging out, standing around, and many of them were smoking. I didn't know what, but that smell was weird and unlike anything I knew. You never forget your first second-hand reefer smoke. Oh, so THAT'S what "Jimmy" was puffing in those health class films.

We got into one of the non-alcohol clubs and it was deafening. A band I had never heard of (and either disappeared into obscurity or Eric Clapton was playing and I just didn't know it) was electrifying the room. This was a much harder-edged sound than I was used to. Piercing guitars and ferocious percussion. I loved the newness of it more than I loved the actual music, but I felt that same twinge I had when I first saw the Beatles on Ed Sullivan.

I asked Craig if he ever heard music like this before and he said, "In Louisville? Are you kidding? I haven't seen *girls* like this before."

The other clubs were so crowded with such long lines that we decided to just bag it. Too much of a hassle. I'd just wait for the Looney Tunes version.

Pandora's Box was a teen club the size of an outhouse perched on a triangular traffic island on the corner of Sunset and Crescent Heights. Crowds became too large and were snarling traffic at that major intersection. So cops tried to enforce a 10:00 PM curfew (good luck) and just close the club. This resulted in a protest rally – a mob of mostly clean-cut teenagers and twentysomethings wearing pullover sweaters and miniskirts. Police broke it up, a riot resulted, and observer Stephen Stills wrote the song "For What It's Worth" about the incident. A month later Sonny & Cher performed at Pandora's Box but not without serious repercussions. They were kicked off a Rose Parade float. It's amazing Sonny Bono ever got elected to public office with that stain on his record.

I was not part of that riot. But I did buy the record.

Get Out of the Street!

KHJ was giving away Ford Mustangs. KFWB was giving away Norelco shavers and Westinghouse irons.

On August 14th I turned 15 1/2 and immediately got my "Learner's Permit" driver's license. This was a great day for me, a terrifying one for anyone in the San Fernando Valley who drove or found themselves within a hundred yards of a street. I guess this is where I should mention I have terrible depth perception. Normally that doesn't get in my way, but when I'm behind the wheel of a moving two-ton box and can hit things at high speed, that can be worrisome. Eventually I would learn to compensate but not before several bumpers and a fence became collateral damage.

My father taught me to drive in the Battleship Impala. His thanks was almost getting killed numerous times. He would take me out to the Fallbrook Square parking lot early on weekend mornings before stores were open and shoppers arrived (not that there were thundering herds waiting to get into J.C. Penney's). I was fine on wide-open empty flat asphalt surfaces. It was roads and streets and inclines that gave me trouble.

My poor dad. He must've felt like a cat in a clothes dryer every time he got in a car with me.

Taft offered a course in driving instruction and I enrolled in that when school resumed in the fall. The course was broken down into two sections. The first ten weeks was "Drivers' *Education*" and the second ten was "Driver's *Training*." Driver's Education was traffic school. State laws interspersed with cautionary movies showing grisly accidents and teenagers with blood pouring out of their ears. Meanwhile, at the Topanga Theater, Dean Martin, as swinging secret agent Matt Helm, was seen maneuvering the same hairpin turns in Monaco that killed Grace Kelly, but was also speeding and sipping a highball. So who to believe?

Driver's Training meant three of us got to actually drive a car (under the watchful eye of an instructor who always smelled like that funny smoke I first detected on the Sunset Strip). For fifteen minutes we'd each take the wheel, and then for a half hour we'd sit in the back and barf with each jarring lurch and turn. But projectile vomiting was a small price to pay for learning how to drive.

Well have fun, fun, fun, until daddy takes the Dramamine away.

Could the Tribe Keep It Down?

In a rare display of extraordinary courage I decided to phone Bev Fine. I was going to ask her about some homework (an ingenious ruse, no?) and if, by some miracle, things went well I might even ask her out to a movie.

So I pick up the phone. Gulp!

After many false starts and mini panic attacks I finally dial her number. "Hello?" It was her dad. No guy in the pre-cell phone era *ever* called a girl without her dad picking up the receiver – the first line of daughter defense. My voice cracked so badly that he mercifully spared me the speech detailing how he'd kill me, my family, and my pets if I so much as touched his precious daughter. He owned a beauty parlor and everyone knows those are not the guys to trifle with.

He put her on the phone. I was actually talking to Bev Fine on the telephone! If only I had picked a different night.

My younger brother, Corey was in the Indian Guides (YMCA's version of the Boy Scouts). Unfortunately, tonight was the "tribe" meeting and it was held at our *teepee*. Fifteen fathers and sons, all in tacky American Indian costumes, were in the next room loudly chanting and marching around the tribe's totem pole in what today would be considered a horribly offensive-bordering-on-appalling activity. One of the dads was a tenured professor at UCLA. If only his students could see him dressed as Tonto waving a tomahawk.

So as I'm trying to talk to Bev and be ultra cool, I'm drowned out by the crazed whoop, "Poconino! Poconino! Who-ya, who-ya, Poconino!" It was like, "Hi, Bev, I'm calling from an insane asylum. Me and the other patients can't figure out the Geometry homework." I was mortified. But God bless, Bev. She thought it was funny. I can only imagine if it had been Dana. Every girl at Taft would be mimicking the war dance as they passed me by.

I didn't ask Bev out—I would have had to scream it, which I decided was not ultra cool – but I was so touched by how sweet she was and how kind she was that a little thing like not humiliating me in front of the entire student body only made me realize that Bev Fine was the absolute love of my life.

Now if only I could tell her before it was too late. But I'm getting ahead of myself.

Be True To Your School

Meanwhile, willowy 19-year-old actress Mia Farrow began dating a "real" senior – Frank Sinatra. He was 49 at the time. It would have been great to double date with them. Maybe go to the Friday night Taft football game, and grab a pizza at Shakey's. You know what else Frank would like? A popular activity among the "in crowd" was TP'ing someone's home. That meant showering the victim's house with streams of toilet paper. I can just imagine Frank hanging with us, tossing a roll, saying this house looked vaguely familiar and then realizing, "Hey, this is where the kidnappers held my son!"

School rivalries were big in the San Fernando Valley, especially in the fall when football reigned supreme. Taft had two rivals – Canoga Park High and Birmingham High. Canoga was our nearest competitor. They had an older stucco campus and a much rougher, uh… *diverse* population. Families routinely avoided buying homes within Canoga Park High's district just to spare their kids from having to be enrolled there. The rivalry would have been bigger had we not been afraid to set foot on the Canoga campus.

So we needed another rival more our socio-economic level. Birmingham High in Encino fit the bill. Good football programs and instead of knife fights; you just had Jews taunting each other that their temples had superior air conditioning.

It usually came down to Taft vs. Birmingham and this year the big game was held there, in their gleaming new stadium. The P.A. announcer was Dick Van Dyke whose son was a member of the "Braves." (Now they're the "Patriots" – don't you just love political correctness? "Poconino! Poconino! Who-ya, who-ya, Poconino!")

We won the big game and the West Valley title. Our road to the City Championship ended however in the first playoff game when Dorsey High (from the "Big K Kingdom") beat us by 50 points. 300-pound future NFL stars proved to be a tougher challenge than Dick Van Dyke's offspring.

The fall semester was also basketball season. Having suffered through basketball boot camp in the spring, I intended to get my just rewards and actually "play" the damn game. I was assigned to the "B" team, which is essentially junior varsity. And I was terrible. Only if there was twelve seconds to go in the game and we were leading by at least 65 points would the coach send me in, and usually with instructions to just stand underneath the basket and let myself get fouled. After maybe three games I was cut from the team. But the coach had a proposition. How would I like to become the varsity manager? I would collect the balls after practice. That seemed very demeaning to me, insulting even. Until I learned it would satisfy my P.E. requirement. Sold! I was team manager for three years. And for the next two springs I was manager of the varsity gymnastics team (same coach) where my chief responsibility was to hand out chalk. Not many people can say they lettered in two varsity sports and never once took a shower.

Receiving a varsity letter meant you could wear a letterman's sweater. So I bought one (they were expensive), wore it proudly one day, and six football players almost stuffed me in a toilet. It seems only *real* athletes were entitled to wear lettermen sweaters. Part of why I agreed to be the manager in the first place was because I liked being considered part of a team. I had never had that experience before. But the football goons graciously set me straight. I was still the outsider; now out fifty bucks for a sweater I could no longer wear.

One very big perk of being a manager during basketball season was that I got to be the P.A. announcer at home games. Since I always wanted to be a sportscaster this was a Godsend. But I was fired from that too when I caused a major incident during the big Taft-Chatsworth game. I thought I saw a Chatsworth player signal a ref so I said, "And Chatsworth wants a time out." The ref heard that and charged a time out to them. Well, the signal was apparently for something else (Ooops. My bad.) and the Chatsworth coach went ballistic. This resulted in a technical for our team. Now our coach was livid. In short order everyone was screaming at everyone else. I spent the rest of the games icing ankles.

Thus concludes the section on my vaunted athletic career in high school. And beyond for that matter.

Football games were usually followed by Friday night dances. I won't belabor this excruciating exercise. Janis Ian made a nice living writing songs about teenage angst at dances and such. But it was a chance to see how much more fun life would have been if I were better looking. Or could dance.

Still, I toughed it out. I just kept telling myself "It's better than Hemet."

Meanwhile, on the *Janis Ian-girl side* of things, it must've been worse. First off, there was now a level playing field. In junior high the early bloomers got attention regardless of looks or personality. But now they *all* had breasts. Bad skin and braces were no longer overlooked for Double D's (well, maybe for Double D's but certainly not B's.)

And decorum dictated that boys had to ask them to dance, not the other way around. So after every two-minute song it was another round of rejection.

One night I spotted one of these undesired girls. She was standing by herself in her ill-fitting party dress. She looked heartbreakingly sad. So I approached and asked her to dance. She told me to go fuck myself. At that exact moment I understood why teenagers drink.

Taft was no different than any high school. There was the caste system. There were cliques. Where you sat in the cafeteria defined your place in the world. I was practically in the parking lot. Everyone wanted to bang the cheerleaders. "Reputations" were important. If you made out with too many boys you were labeled a slut. Good girls lived in mortal fear of guys bragging (which they all did). One good girl ingeniously got around this problem by sleeping with her brother.

Cheerleaders, of course, were royalty. Personally, I never understood the concept of cheerleading. Who really gives a shit if the Neanderthals jocks—who are taking all the girls you covet— beat some other Cro-Magnons in varsity football? Cheer your own damn boyfriends. Why should I join the chorus?

My classes that semester included English Literature taught by a woman who must've dated Chaucer. Geometry, taught by a very attractive young babe who only had one arm. Chemistry, where I was introduced to the magic of the Periodic Table. I think I had history. I don't remember. Drivers' Ed, Gymnastics ("Damn it, Levine, where's the chalk?!"), and my elective was "Art Production." We painted banners and posters for upcoming school events. Imagine getting class credit for tagging!

My beloved Dodgers got into the World Series against the Minnesota Twins, but Sandy Koufax refused to pitch the opening game. It was scheduled for Yom Kippur, the Jewish High Holiday. This made Koufax the hero of every Jewish kid, myself included. Don Drysdale pitched that first game instead and got shelled. When manager Walt Alston came out to the mound to lift him, Don said, "Yeah, yeah, I know what you're thinking. Why couldn't *he* be Jewish?" Koufax did pitch… several games including the dramatic 7th game clincher on only two day's rest.

Like everyone else in Los Angeles, I was enthralled by Dodger announcer Vin Scully. Not everyone else wanted to *be* Vin Scully however. I did. I think I can trace my love of baseball, storytelling, the English language, and Farmer John all-beef hot dogs to Vin Scully. I owe several careers and my chronic acid reflux to that man.

The End of the '50s

Icouldn't fathom why anyone would watch the Andy Williams variety show on NBC if they didn't own a color TV. It was so wholesome your teeth ached. Whatever "edge" the show had was provided by the Osmond Family. But it was in color and production numbers always featured grinning All-American kids in brightly colored sweaters holding brightly colored balloons. Not having a color TV and not being gay I never watched *The Andy Williams Show*... except...

When it was time for the annual Christmas special.

Andy would always have his beautiful family on the show. Mrs. Williams & Andy and the adorable towheads would sing Carols, exchange presents, and their message of love and holiday good cheer would melt even the coldest heart. That's not why I watched it, of course. I wanted to screw Andy's wife.

Claudine Longet (Mrs. W.) was a willowy brunette with exquisite doe eyes and luscious lips. Laura Petrie but French. She was also a successful recording artist but believe me, if she looked like Charles De Gaulle she couldn't give away one record. But I found her incredibly sexy, even when she was singing Silent Night in front of a crucifix. She and Andy divorced in the '70s and two years later she shot her boyfriend, Olympic skier Spider Sabich to death. I stopped wanting to screw her then.

I'll be on parole for Christmas.

Dad's annual Miline Club Christmas Show was a big hit. I wasn't allowed to attend because they felt it was inappropriate for a 15-year-old boy to see a naked stripper. I guess seeing my father in bloomers doing the Can-Can was not objectionable.

1965 was really the last year of the 1950's. We still thought and acted like we were in *The Donna Reed Show* or *Ozzie and Harriet.* There was an innocence that steadfastly persisted despite pesky flashes of reality – riots, a war, civil unrest, drugs, and teen rebellion.

But we were growing more and more uneasy, to the point where my generation had to finally take action: So we sang.

My peers could not have a thought or a feeling or bowel movement without singing about it. Out of this unrest came "the protest song." Bob Dylan and Joan Baez were the vanguards, but the tune that perhaps had the biggest impact was "Eve of Destruction" by Barry McGuire. Barry McGuire had been the lead singer of The New Christy Minstrels, a wholesome collection of apple-cheeked, young goody-gooders who sang about hayrides and gooseberry preserves. McGuire veered somewhat from the hootenanny by singing a tale of imminent world doom. Within weeks it was the number one record in the country. Written by P.F. Sloan, the lyrics were filled with cheery bon mots like "the world is exploding," bodies are floating in the Jordan River, the button could be pushed at any moment, and the world will soon be in a grave. De-lightful!

The song fed directly into the terror and foreboding fear we all lived with every single day… although it wasn't so terrifying that we didn't buy the record and dance to it at parties.

In truth it was more like the Eve of *Distraction*. At least for me. It was hard enough to focus on my own self-centered little life with all the changes that were about to take place.

Before POW Meant Prisoner of War

My generation – we were collectively the *Prettiest Girl In Town*. And all the *Gentleman Callers* (Hollywood, Madison Avenue, GM) did back flips to win our favor. And like the prettiest girl, after awhile we just took it for granted. *Of course* everyone catered to us; we were special. We were destined to do great things. Our parents and our teachers and the American Broadcasting Company said so.

In 1966 ABC was the distant third network behind CBS and NBC. So in an attempt to carve out their own niche they geared their programming primarily to us. We were the largest generation the world had ever known, after all. And we were the first to grow up with television. The way to reach us was through that flickering tube. Television was boomer flypaper.

ABC couldn't sell ratings but they could sell demographics. Ironically, today *all* that's important are demographics. 18-34 is the only age group the networks (and advertisers in general) care about. You could have huge numbers, but if the viewers were all my age, today the networks couldn't give a shit.

It's been a rude shock when those same *Gentleman Callers* no longer have the remotest interest in us *Prettiest Girls in Town...*

even as *Cougars.*

While CBS offered grown-up favorites like Jackie Gleason, Lucille Ball, and Andy Griffith and NBC featured relics Bob Hope and Dean Martin, the ABC stable of stars read like the Beverly Hills High drama club. Patty Duke, Shelley Fabares, Sally Field, and Ricky Nelson. *Shindig* was on two nights a week. The youth-oriented shows were popular but none really became breakout hits.

Until January 12, 1966

That's the night *Batman* premiered.

It instantly became my new favorite show. Me and everyone else under 20. "Camp" and "kitsch" were the zeitgeist of the day and the Caped Crusader was its superhero. Fight scenes were punctuated with on-screen comic book words POW! BAM! ZONK! The Caped Crusader was played by an actor who had the agility of a hunchback. But Adam West's goofy sincerity struck just the right chord and this tongue-in-cheek comedy was an instant smash (Sorry. I meant SMASH!).

You look back at those old *Batman* episodes and think, "What schlock!" And in fairness, by season two we thought that too. By the time Otto Preminger played a villain, we had moved on.

Grades came out in January. I was a B+ student (thanks in large part to that A I got in P.E. for distributing towels). It was crucial I did well in school. I didn't want my parents to say I couldn't listen to KHJ while doing 11th Grade homework. You could win a console color TV and meet the stars of *Batman.* (I suppose Batman was KHJ's answer to KFXM's *Hooded Rapist.*)

KHJ also introduced a new disc jockey, Tommy Vance, who was British. The British Invasion was still in full-force. Everything girls wore was "*Piccadilly*" this and "*Liverpool*" that. Competitor KFWB countered with Lord Tim, another Brit. One night Tommy Vance mysteriously disappeared. Turns out he got his draft notice and just fled the country. "*I won't be in tonight, mate. I'm in Europe.*" Tommy Vance was two years ahead of the curve.

With the war in Vietnam escalating, the draft board needed more bodies. By 1966, marriage and fatherhood deferments outnumbered student deferments by nearly two-to-one. Fearing the backlash that would occur if the selective service board discontinued student deferments it instead severely restricted fatherhood free passes and eliminated the marriage deferment. As the clock struck midnight on the day that would eliminate the marriage loophole there were 20,000 weddings. That's a lot of blenders to be returned at one time.

The other reason to do well scholastically in the 11th grade was that my entire future depended upon it. Grades and SAT scores determined which college you got into. The low end was Pierce Jr. College, known as Cow Tech (for its agricultural program not coeds) and the high end was UCLA and USC. Very few Southern California kids traveled out of state in 1966. Maybe you'd enroll at UC Berkeley or Stanford, but if you wanted to be really adventurous and go back east you applied to Arizona State.

My university of choice was UCLA. Actually it was my *parents'* university of choice, but through insidious brainwashing techniques like taking me to UCLA football and basketball games, they got me to drink the Kool-Aid. Still, I had to get accepted. So this was the year I was prepared to knuckle-down… as long as it didn't interfere with my cartooning and entering Batman contests.

You Don't Say

I turned 16 on Valentine's Day. This is a bigger milestone for girls. Guys do not have Sweet Sixteen parties. They just get their driver's license.

Unless they have no depth perception, took the exam in a Chevy Impala the size of an aircraft carrier, and failed the test miserably. Happy birthday to me.

The worst part was that I had to wait several weeks to re-take the exam. So everybody *knew* I failed. To save face – because how humiliating to say you couldn't parallel park – I just said I hit a guy.

After much practice, re-taking the test in my mom's Mercury Comet (a car that could fit in the Impala's glove compartment), I finally passed and got that elusive passport to freedom.

Which meant I finally went out on a real first date. I was still way too intimidated to ask Bev Fine so I asked Marcy Loudon. I wanted to get a few rejections under my belt first so I could better withstand Bev's ultimate lethal blow. Amazingly, Marcy said yes and that Saturday night I took her to the Corbin Theater on Ventura Blvd. to see one of the great date movies of all-time, *To Kill*

A Mockingbird.

The plan was to put my arm around her about halfway into the film. It was tough though finding just that right moment in the rape trial. I think I got up the courage and draped my arm around her just as Tom is shot to death while trying to escape from jail.

For a nightcap I took Marcy to Farrell's Ice Cream parlor where we discussed the differences between the movie and the book, and I had her home by midnight. A quick peck on the cheek and that was it. She retired for the night, probably thinking what a nice polite boy I was. I meanwhile, went home and jacked off to her.

All girls had curfews back then. Midnight was standard. The penalty for violation was usually grounding. Grounding was actually an effective deterrent in 1966 – at least for the girls *I* dated. I'm sure my classmate who slept with own her brother didn't give a shit if she couldn't go to the Spring Sing. But the girls I dated always *insisted* on being home by twelve. And I choose to believe it was because of that severe penalty. Please allow me that little fantasy.

Just as getting your drivers license is a rite of passage, so is your first auto accident. I experienced both in the same week. I had taken Terry Levy to NBC in Burbank to watch the taping of the game show *You Don't Say* with Tom Kennedy. Terry Levy, by the way, is my de facto sister. We're only a month apart in age and have known each other our entire lives. We lived next door when we were infants and we've always been close. A few weeks earlier, her family moved nearby (right behind Flooky's hot dog stand on Ventura Blvd., a *prime* location), and I helped Terry assimilate into Taft.

Within a week she had more friends than I did. And like any good sister, she played matchmaker—setting me up with a number of her new friends. I can honestly say that any girl Terry introduced me to was nuts. But Eleanor and the others are for later.

The accident. It was just a minor scrape getting out of the NBC parking lot. But the combination of the U.S.S. Impala and a Cyclops behind the wheel resulted in a number of these fender benders. My savings bonds rapidly disappeared into the hands of body shop owners. Terry was very sweet, in that sisterly way. "This could happen to anybody," she said. But before I could thank her added, "Just don't do it on a date."

WKRP In Woodland Hills

Our high school made national news in March!

The March 21ˢᵗ edition of *Newsweek* magazine did their big cover story on "The Teenagers – a Newsweek survey of what they're really like" and a good portion of it focused on Taft High. The cover featured a pretty coed sitting on the back of a motorcycle, glancing over her shoulder at the camera. That girl was Taft senior, Jan Smithers. Jan, of course, would go on to play Bailey on *WKRP In Cincinnati*.

The survey determined that there was, in fact, a so-called "Generation Gap" (who knew???). And it was widening because the older generation was resistant to listening to and understanding us. Whatever. *Taft* was mentioned! And our very own Jan was selected as the cover girl!

For five minutes she was the absolute star of the school, eclipsing even the football star, and the girl who played a burn victim on *Ben Casey*.

The cover itself was very telling. Yes, we were rebellious. Yes we rode motorcycles. But they were cute little putt-putts with drivers who wore jean jackets and California golden girls on the back who wore sweaters and white slacks. Not exactly leather and chains and skull tattoos.

I had fifteen seconds of fame myself in May when I was a finalist to win the KHJ Birthday Firebird. For their one-year anniversary they invited listeners to submit homemade birthday cards and selected one per hour to qualify to win a new Pontiac Firebird. I drew caricatures of all the disc jockeys and one magic Tuesday night Johnny Mitchell announced my name. The next day you would think I was actually *popular*. People were stopping me in the hall, congratulating me. Even one of the shop majors said, "Way to go, faggot." By the next day I was completely forgotten. And when I didn't win, the only consolation I received was a few kids saying they knew all along I never had a chance cause I was a fucking dork.

But, oh, that one day...

The Meanest and Ugliest Teacher in the School

That's how Mr. Solkovits introduced himself on our first day in his American History class. I had been warned about Mr. Solkovits. Supposedly the hardest teacher at Taft.

My classmates were sweating like whores in church, but I thought, "Wait a minute. This guy's not ugly. He looks like Tyrone Power. He's goofing with us." I liked him instantly. And yes he was tough. But also the best teacher I ever had. High school, college – no one came close. His lectures were enthralling. He really made history come alive. I loved his class. But…

Jesus, his tests were brutal.

You couldn't just memorize. You had to actually *think*. (No wonder everyone despised him.) And if you did poorly he would dropkick your paper up the aisle to you. He would also spring pop quizzes called "Knuckleheads vs. Brains." The boys lined up on one side of the room and the girls on the other, and Solkovits, like a game show host, would fire us questions. The side that won (Brains) each got five extra points on the next test. Today this would be considered so politically incorrect he'd be up on charges, but then it was just good clean sexist fun.

I busted my ass and got an A in his class. There were very few of us. Five total for all his classes. He told all of us A students to be in front of the school at 6:30 that upcoming Wednesday (but wouldn't say why). He rolled up in a station wagon and took us all to a Dodger game. How cool is that? Short of singing "To Sir With Love," thanks Mr. Solkovits.

The winning pitcher that night was Larry Dierker, former Taft alum.

Taft was quite the professional athlete mill in those days. A number of big leaguers were former Toreadors. In addition to Dierker, Rick Auerbach, hall-of-famer Robin Yount, Kevin Kennedy, and Pete Lacock all wore the proud Toreador jersey.

Lacock was also notable for being the son of Peter Marshall, host of the NBC game show *Hollywood Squares,* and his sister Suzy went out with me a couple of times that semester. I must've really made a big impression. Years later I bumped into her and she refused to acknowledge she even knew me. Even after I described her dad's office in great detail she still maintained I didn't look familiar. Christ! Would it have killed her to *lie?* It's amazing that you can be ten, twenty, thirty years removed from high school, but one incident like that and bam! You're right back there, feeling that same sickening pit in your stomach, that same crushing rejection.

Happily, not every girl forgot me. In fact, there were a couple that not only remembered me but remembered details that never occurred. Like at my last high school reunion. A girl approached me and recalled how much fun we had when we dated each other. Now, I have an excellent memory of which girls went out with me, and which did not, and this girl definitely did not.

I wasn't sure how to handle this moment. I figured she wouldn't just make that up knowing I could call her on it.

What I think happened was this: She saw my name frequently on television. She started telling her friends that *she knew me*, and that evolved into *we dated,* and eventually we were *boy and girlfriend.* She told that story enough times that eventually she started actually believing it herself. I thought back to Suzy Lacock and didn't want to be a dick so I just said, "Yes, those were good times" and politely made my exit. Afterwards, I thought, "that was lame; there has to be a better response" and a moment or two later I came up with one. But it was too late of course.

An hour later, wouldn't you know? The exact same thing happened with another girl who back in the day wouldn't pee on my head if my hair was on fire. Now she was going on and on to a group of people about how much fun we had going out together. This time I was ready. I agreed that it was wonderful then took her hand and wistfully said, "Y'know, you were only the second girl I ever slept with." "Huh?!" she said in abject horror. I moved off, and for the rest of the night, every time I would spot her across the room she had the same thoroughly puzzled look.

Oh, if only I had said that to Suzy Lacock. Although how much worse for me would it have been if I really *did* sleep with Suzy Lacock and she still didn't remember me?

Working With an Ocelot and a Cricket

"Dead Man's Curve," Jan & Dean's catchy hit tune about driving too fast and crashing horribly became all too real. On April 12th, Jan (Berry) was seriously injured when he totaled his Corvette, hitting a parked car on Whittier Blvd, about two blocks from "Dead Man's Curve" on Sunset Blvd.

As red-blooded L.A. teens, we were wrapped up in the lore and romance of street drag racing. Beach Boys songs about *409's* and *Little Deuce Coupes* "shutting down" other guys were all the rage. I'd sing along with these auto anthems and have no idea what I was talking about. What the hell is a "flat head mill" or "Lake Pipes" or "Pressure Plates?"

But this was all part of my participating in popular activities without actually doing anything. *Drag racing* was Natural Selection as it applied to Auto Shop majors. *Surfing* was being shot out of a cannon in the ocean. So I knew the lingo, read the magazines, bought the records but only drove 15 MPH on Dead Man's Curve and only saw "gnarly waves" and "Banzai Pipelines" in Bruce Brown's superb documentary *Endless Summer* (which I saw at the Elks Hall in Reseda).

Instead, I filled my days engrossed in radio, cartooning, doing errands for mom so I could use the car (1966 prices: Folger's Coffee, two-pound can—$1.45, Asparagus, $.25 a pound, Pork Chops, $.69 a pound.), dropping my little brother Corey off at his various baseball/soccer/football/basketball practices and occasionally remembering to pick him up, tying my self worth to the fate and fortunes of the Dodgers (fortunately they were good that year), and looking for an after-school job. With all my little fender benders, an infusion of cash was imperative.

To be more precise, I needed a *second* job. I drew a comic strip for the monthly Woodland Hills newspaper. *Rock Roll*, the story of a typical American teenager who was popular because he played a magic harmonica. This paid $5.00 a month, and eventually I was let go for budgetary reasons. Apparently major syndicates were strapped too because even at that low price, none of them were willing to pick up this can't-miss strip.

I applied for a job as an usher at the Baronet Theater. This was one of those new "art" theaters that were popping up. They showed foreign movies with subtitles, black & white independent films, and were all the size of shoeboxes wedged into neighborhood shopping centers. But even though they seated maybe fifty people, there were never any lines for *Andrei Rublev*. Especially when *Godzilla vs. the Sea Monster* was playing at the nearby Topanga Theater. I wasn't hired. They didn't need an usher. They needed a colony of French people to settle in Tarzana.

Making my rounds at the Topanga Plaza one Saturday morning in August of '66 I encountered the manager of Wallichs Music City as he was opening for the day. "Why should I hire you?" he asked. "Because I know every record in your store and every artist, " I said. (Usually I'm not that brazen or quick). "You start Thursday," he said.

I was THRILLED! My first job. Five hours on Thursdays and seven on Saturdays. For $1.15 an hour (minimum wage). I ran home and excitedly told my father. He was very proud of me. Then he said, "So no more allowance after this week."

Wha?

ME: "Wait a minute. If I have to work to make the same money I would've made just by doing nothing, why should I work?"

DAD: "Because that money is *yours*. You earned it and no one has any say in what you do with it. If you want to spend it all on records or pinball machines or whatever, that's your business. If I give you the money that's a different story."

That sold me. I valued the independence. Before you applaud me for being so mature, my first thought was " Now I can save up for a hooker."

Considering that my classmates were all boxing groceries or changing the grease traps at McDonald's, I considered myself extremely lucky to be hawking 45's.

I manned the singles counter. That meant I helped customers, restocked the bins, and let people into the listening booths. Just like in the Hollywood store, you could sample albums for free. A lot of rock bands lived in nearby Topanga Canyon and less-nearby Laurel Canyon and would slither down the hill to check out the competition. The great Captain Beefheart was a Wallichs regular!

We had one rule: no smoking pot. We didn't want the 70-year-old grandmother to get a contact high following Captain Beefheart in the booth, not to mention those glass cubicles served as the store window. Public displays of illegal behavior were bad for the store's image.

The biggest transgressor was the Buffalo Springfield's Neil Young.

And he was a shithead. I used to throw him out once a week. Plus, he slept with and dumped a girl I had a crush on so I took every opportunity to kick his raggedy ass to the curb.

Two notable co-workers: Steve Hall, who went on to become a world-renowned pianist/ recording artist and died way too young. And Skip, who frequently brought his pet ocelot to work. I pleaded with Skip to lock it in a listening booth with Neil Young.

Night managers would come and go. These were usually alcoholics who owned decent suits. They'd generally last about three months. One night manager we had for awhile, who was not on the sauce was Nik Sullivan. I once asked him what he did before this and he modestly confessed he played guitar in a group. I said, "Really? Which group? Any one I've heard of?" He said, "Yeah, Buddy Holly and the Crickets." "Oh bullshit!" I said. He shrugged, meandered over to the Buddy Holly section, pulled out an album, and son of a bitch, there he was.

Talk about being extremely lucky. He escaped death twice. First when he decided not to board that doomed flight that took Holly's life, and second when I let a robber into his office who had a gun.

In fairness, I didn't know he was a robber. Hey, he didn't wear a mask. I was thrown. Instead, he wore a tailored suit and said he was the manager of the Hollywood branch. He had done his homework. He knew Nik's name. So when he asked if Nik was in the office I said, "Sure, go on back." He walked out five minutes later with a week's receipts after pointing a loaded pistol at Nik's head. Where is an ocelot when you need one?

Nik didn't blame me, said anyone in my place would have done the same thing; still it's always nagged at me that I almost got a Cricket killed.

On the other hand, he was the only cricket I *didn't* want killed that spring.

May was the month of the *Great Cricket Invasion*.

Maybe it was due to the winter rain. I dunno. But our idyllic tract community became infested with crickets. Ignoring screen doors, the Nike missiles and signs on the front lawn saying we were protected by Westinghouse Security, thousands of them managed to infiltrate everyone's house. You'd take a step in the bathroom and "*crunch*!"

The nights were the worst. You'd hear a loud steady roar of them chirping, sometimes from under (or inside!) your bed. Needless to say, nobody slept. So after maybe five or six nights our neighborhood was like *The Walking Dead*. People wandered around in a daze, tempers were short, the smell of bug spray was everywhere. This lasted several months until they either went to Cancun for the winter or the smog got to them too.

Smog was a huge issue in Los Angeles in 1966. Before there were emission controls, cars just coughed out sooty exhaust. With no rain to wash it away, by the late summer a visible brown haze engulfed the city – especially in pockets like Pasadena where the air was trapped by the San Gabriel Mountains. Weather forecasts included smog levels (light, moderate, heavy, Pompeii).

This could not have been good for our lungs, but of course we were young and if respiratory problems developed in thirty or forty years, so what? That was like *forever*.

Major efforts were made to control auto exhaust and regulate factories. In the '60s it was routine to have over 120 stage-one smog days. (By 1996 that number dropped to seven. Of course that could also be due to eight less Chevy Impalas on the road.)

In Other News:

- Thousands of Americans continued to die in Vietnam, but the country went into mourning when President Johnson's beagle was run over by a White House car while chasing a squirrel.

- The first telephone answering machine was invented. It was the size and weight of an anvil.

- The Beatles new album *Yesterday and Today* was released in June and then quickly recalled. The cover showed the lovable mop tops in white smocks with dismembered plastic babies and slabs of meat. In a few years, rock groups would be biting the heads off of chickens and killing goats live on stage, but for the summer of 1966, uncooked liver was not appropriate for our delicate eyes.

- In the last week of school, Bev Fine announced that she and her family were moving to New York. I was crushed. First Ann; now Bev. Is it possible to have abandonment issues if the person leaving doesn't realize they're abandoning you?

Ann went to Catholic school so I blamed the Catholics. Bev's family was relocating to be near her brother who was studying to become a rabbi. So this was the Jews' fault. Thank God there were no Mormon girls at Taft. I don't think I could have handled the next love of my life leaving me for missionary work in Suriname.

As with Ann, I retreated to my room for several weeks of being distraught. This is what teenagers did back then. In addition to "In My Room" I now had another self-pity anthem to enjoy during my wallowing—"I Am a Rock" by Simon & Garfunkel. In this ditty someone is locked away in his room, shrouded in gloom, isolating himself from the world like a rock or island because inanimate objects don't feel pain or cry.

See? I wasn't just heartbroken. I was also *complex!*

And they say teenage girls are hyper emotional and overly dramatic. I did everything but light candles and cover my windows with black crepe.

Songs on the radio meant so much to me because well, I had no other life. Certain songs I identified with certain people. For Bev Fine it was "Cherish" by the Association. A heartsick guy doesn't have the guts to confess his feelings to the girl he "cherishes," while watching all these other, unfit suitors feed her bullshit lines and hope to just get in her pants.

I think you see the connection.

The school year ended. Bev signed my yearbook and was gone. But to this day, whenever I hear that song on an oldies station, I immediately think of her and feel a pang of sadness.

I still have that yearbook. Here's what some of my classmates wrote about me. A few I can't identify. They just signed their first names, like I would never encounter another Dave or Jennifer in my entire life.

Ken
To one of the best artists I know of. Thank you for helping me with my posters and stuff. Good luck the next semester.
–Cathy

Ken
I sure had fun this semester watching you draw all those little characters! Best of luck
–Jennifer

Ken
Even though Birmingham's a better school – I met a lot of nice people here – you are one – Thanks.
–Delinda

Ken
I've known you for a long time, maybe longer.
–Bonnie

Ken
Keep your head out of the way of low flying turtles & Goodyear blimps & don't let your meat loaf & have a good time in the summer.
–Dave

Ken
How are you! Fine while I look at ya. Hope you're in my classes next semester! If you're "not," (gack, ugh!) well tough! Love 'n' stuff.
–Ramona

(note: this is the girl who slept with her brother)

Ken
You're so nice. I think you're very talented so good luck in your future.
Best wishes

– Chris

Get the picture? I'm nice, I can draw, I help people with their posters. I'm not getting laid until I'm 50. No one signed "*Love*" except one.

Ken,
Best of luck to one of the best agents a star could ever have. Think of the deep satisfaction you'll get when you see my name in lights (I'm very handy with a flashlight). Thanks anyway – you tried. (even if I didn't become an overnight sensation.)
Love,
Bev Fine

"Cherish is the word." Have a nice life, Bev.

The Big Kahuna

1966 was the "Summer of the Big Kahuna" – KHJ's most creative and ambitious promotion yet. They created this mythical character, "The Big Kahuna," who legend had it, was on a worldwide search to find some Hawaiian princess' precious stone that was taken from her flaming temple or something. Los Angeles was his next destination (guess he had no luck in Tulsa). Along the way he'd be making personal appearances, giving away money, and be the centerpiece for several contests.

With great fanfare the Big Kahuna arrived at LAX. He was this large Hawaiian aborigine adorned in fur, and beads, and shells, and feathers. (In truth he was a crazy German whose father built the bunker Hitler died in.)

LA kids went along with the conceit. (This was the crap we concerned ourselves with while soldiers were dying in Vietnam.) We flocked to the Big Kahuna's appearances. Forget that he was selling weed out of the back of the KHJ prize van at high schools; the Big Kahuna became a local sensation. We followed his exploits on the air, saw him when we could, bought dope when we were out, and scrambled to be the ninth caller when we heard the "Kahuna cockatoo" or some such nonsense. Winners were entitled to attend the big beach luau, and here's how different things were then: the invitations that KHJ sent out were actual coconuts. You were allowed to send full size coconuts through the U.S. Mail!

Unlike previous summers, I was not bored out of my mind that year. I could borrow the car to drive to the beach occasionally. I could hop a ride with others who were going to the beach. I was still afraid of tight parking spaces, heavy traffic, and venturing "over the hill" so I passed when I had a chance to see the Beatles' at Dodger Stadium. It wasn't worth it.

That was the last local concert they would ever perform.

No family vacation that year, not that we could go very far anyway. 35,000 airline workers from five major carriers went on strike, crippling the industry. From July 8th to August 19th, the peak summer travel season, 60% of U.S. commercial flights were grounded. And it was *still* easier to fly than it is today.

I had my part-time job at Wallichs and got another part-time gig as well. This one ushering at the Valley Music Theater.

The Valley Music Theater on Ventura Blvd. was a huge concrete white shell, very modernistic, very *JFK airport terminal.*

The big musical theater fad in Los Angeles in 1966 was theater-in-the-round. Who needed Broadway when Angelinos could be treated to smash hit musicals of the past with knock-off casts, no sets, and no piece of scenery taller than their ankles? In the LA area there were three venues – the Melodyland Theater in Anaheim (across from the Dopey section of the Disneyland parking lot), the Valley Music Theater in Woodland Hills (later to become the home of the Jehovah's Witnesses), and the Carousel Theater in glamorous West Covina (gateway to the Inland Empire). The productions would bicycle this circuit, usually for two-week runs.

I showed people to their seats at the Valley Music Theater and could not wait for each new show to bring jaw-dropping performances by miscast actors. Dance numbers tended not to be very elaborate since the stage was the size of a conference table. (If they had lasted long enough to do *The Lord Of The Dance,* they would use three guys.)

Headliners tended to be of the B variety. Instead of Henry Fonda, Marlon Brando, and Julie Andrews we got Dennis Day, Frank Gorshin, and Betsy Palmer (best known as a perky game show panelist and knife-wielding crazy in *Friday the 13th: Part Two*).

After several years of burning through the Broadway catalogue the trend petered out. By 1968 they were down to *It's A Bird, It's A Plane, It's Superman* starring local TV news anchors.

Still, I was able to see beyond the *game show-celebrity-guest-caliber* casts and really appreciate the writing. That summer I also read Moss Hart's autobiography *Act One* and was intrigued by the notion of being a New York playwright. It all sounded so romantic to me – writing all night in a hotel room in exotic New Haven, getting a brainstorm, and saving a play at the last minute, opening on Broadway, having a hit…and someday seeing my work performed at the Valley Music Theater by Barbara Walters.

Of course I didn't only usher musicals. The Indianapolis 500 auto race was a huge annual event. But back then there was no network television coverage of it. You either listened to "the greatest spectacle of racing" on the radio anchored by Sid Collins, or you went to selected theaters to watch a closed circuit feed. The Valley Music Theater was offering the telecast and I volunteered to be one of the ushers. Hey, they were paying $2.50 an hour! I believe the race started at 8:00 AM on the west coast. All I know is we started letting people in at 6:30. By 7:00 AM the place was packed. There were numerous full bars going from the moment the doors opened.

USC football players were hired as the bartenders, just to make sure things didn't get too out of hand.

The race started and literally within the first ten seconds there was a fourteen-car pile up. Roadsters were caroming off each other, smashing into the wall, catching fire, tires flying, drivers scurrying, some scaling the fence. Fortunately, no one was seriously hurt. But the race was halted for another hour-and-a-half. Needless to say, the natives were getting restless... and hammered. By the time the drivers rounded the very first turn, 3,000 boisterous rowdies had been drinking for three hours. The next six hours were insane. There was almost a riot when they ran out of snacks. It was not uncommon to see someone vomiting. Me and three other ushers tried to break up a fight and I got punched. I think it was someone from my temple.

The race finally ended and these lushes staggered out to their cars. God knows how any of them made it home – if they *did*. We ushers had to comb the building to make sure everyone was out. Yeah, big concern that some were going to hide in the bathrooms for five hours so they could sneak into that night's performance of *The World of Susie Wong* starring Connie Chung.

Hey, Hey, They're the Monkees

The big sensations of 1966 so far were Batman and the Big Kahuna. In keeping with that theme of teen idols that were complete fabrications, the Monkees were born.

The Monkees were a total Hollywood invention. The group wasn't formed, it was cast. Producers had sold a sitcom pilot to NBC about a musical group like the early Beatles – fun loving and zany. Whether they were good musicians was immaterial. Their music would be produced in the studio. More important was how they *looked* together. Covering their bases they hired one British kid, a former child actor, a musician of sorts, and someone who was just plain goofy. By-the-numbers casting. Everything about this group was manufactured, artificial, and bogus.

Within a month they were a national phenomenon. Their rise was so meteoric and their popularity so off-the-charts that even the Beatles were eclipsed. Score one for Corporate America.

Their records were selected for them, written by proven hit makers like Carole King and Neil Diamond, backed up by studio musicians, and produced and arranged by industry heavyweights. Originally the four Monkees were so bad that each had to be recorded separately. But the records that resulted were pure magic. Score two for Corporate America.

Their debut single was "Last Train to Clarksville," and lest you think I was above getting caught up in this Monkee Machiavellian mania, I loved the record the minute I heard it. I bought it from Montgomery Wards the day it arrived at Wallichs.

I must say that the only aspect of the Monkees I didn't like was their television show. Not funny for a second. Their attempts at physical comedy were woeful. It was amateur night in Dixie. And yet, any other four guys (even if they were gifted comedians) and the whole Monkees craze probably wouldn't have happened. That's the genius… or dumb luck of the whole phenomenon.

Make no mistake – we weren't just the "Pepsi Generation," we were the "Gullible Generation." We were impressionable teens that played right into Madison Avenue's hands. Or NBC's.

Yet all that was soon to change. They could sell us Stridex Medicated Pads, Little Hondas, Coppertone, Heaven Scent, "the California Myth," and "the British Invasion." They could sell us Batman and the Monkees. But they couldn't sell us Vietnam.

Not that they didn't try. "The Ballad of the Green Berets" by Marine Sergeant Barry Sadler was the rallying call for the "hawks" (pro-war, generally older). They found this message stirring and powerful. Be one of America's best, give your life for those oppressed – that sort of thing. The song concludes with a Green Beret dying and his last request is that his son someday becomes a Green Beret as well. Gee, thanks, pop!

Thousands enlisted because of this idiotic song.

By mid-summer there were 290,000 U.S. soldiers in Vietnam. Playing "Six Degrees of Separation," with a number that large, it didn't take long before everyone in the country was touched personally by someone associated with the war. Excuse me, "police action." The government wouldn't even acknowledge it as a war. Their official term was "police action." That's like calling the Spanish Inquisition a "Fact Finding" expedition.

If there was a generation gap before, this issue really widened it. Within a couple of years the chasm would become as large as the Grand Canyon.

Looking back...

Corey, Dad, and me in my idiotic green jacket. 1966

Our house before finishing touches. April, 1960.

Our house. January, 1961

Our house. June, 2012

Living in suburbia. August, 1961

My first car – A 1960 Comet.

The U.S.S. Chevy Impala

Mom & Dad on Zuma Beach.
July, 1965

The Taft High Drill Team.
Maybe two of these girls went out with me.

The Dating Game –
One of the bachelorettes
who didn't choose me.

Me, Nana Lil, Grampy Sid,
Mom, Dad, Corey and Babette.
1967

PART THREE

French Girls

We got a dog that summer. A poodle-terrier. My mother named her.

Babette.

That name would not have been my choice. I don't remember why we got a dog. We never had a pet before. But I was thrilled. And Babs turned out to be a fabulous dog and companion. If someone in the house were sick, she'd sit all day at the end of his bed. I worried that our family, unaccustomed to caring for pets might not take the best care of her – and my early fears were justified.

Our house was only two blocks from the Woodland Hills Park. On the 4th of July, they would shoot off fireworks. We always invited a few people over for a barbeque and fireworks show, comfortably viewed from our backyard. A neighbor was lying on a chaise lounge. He set his martini down on the ground. Babette approached and lapped up the entire contents in mere seconds. Ten minutes later she staggered out onto the lawn and passed out for twenty-four hours. We have a dog for one month and get her completely shit-faced. Nice.

But eventually, we provided her with such a good home that Grampy Sid once said, "When I die I want to come back as that goddamn dog." Nana Lil also took to Babette. She'd put a little dollop of chopped liver on a matzoth square and serve it to her on a napkin.

Age 16 was a big turning point in my relationship with my brother, Corey. We used to fight constantly. And either I matured or we both just started liking the same shows on the TV we shared, but for the first time we became uneasy friends. We put aside our differences (he resented that I was Mr. Goal Oriented and I had problems with him being a good athlete and normal) and started really appreciating each other. And one thing we definitely could agree upon was our love for Babette. Maybe she was the sibling we both always wanted the other to be.

Alcohol was the drug of choice for my parents' generation. My folks were no more than social drinkers, but every night my father would come home and he and Mom would have a cocktail. Their get-togethers with friends would often be *cocktail parties*. To my knowledge these gin-soaked soirees never led to what we heard were *key parties*. Husbands would drop their car keys in a bowl and at the end of the night wives would reach into the bowl and go to bed with whoever's key they selected. The closest I could see that happening among my parents' friends was all the wives putting their keys in the bowl and then going home with each other to play Pan.

Pan (short for Panguingue) is a rummy card game for four to eight players. It's played with eight decks with the 8's, 9's, and 10's removed. And sometimes a complete set of spades is also removed. How the hell they played this and WHY is still a mystery to me. It's the card game equivalent of Australian Rules Football. But several times a week my mother and her card shark friends would play and smoke and eat doughnuts. (Today they'd take Pilate classes.)

My father's leisure-time activities were golf, poker, and of course cross-dressing for the Miline Club show.

Getting back to the *key party* notion—I was finding myself increasingly attracted to some of my parents' friends (who, like my parents, were in their 30's). It seemed strange, but I figured, if I'm already masturbating to Laura Petrie it's just a short leap to banging my mother's best friend, Mrs. Nussbaum. I seriously thought I had a problem, but not serious enough to stop... or even curtail to three times a week.

Much of my so-called sex education was derived from reading Henry Miller's *Tropic of Cancer*, which my parents had in the family bookshelf along with the Bobbsey Twins and Nancy Drew collections. When my folks were out for the evening and my brother was asleep I headed straight to the "tropic." Sure, I had to slog through ideas and imagery, yada yada, but along the way there was unbelievably explicit sex. And I would imagine me as Henry Miller and the whores as girls from the Taft Drama Club. Or Mrs. Nussbaum.

One day I read in the paper that a new French movie was opening called *The Game Is Over*. The review mentioned that Jane Fonda starred and was naked in quite a few scenes. This I HAD to see! It was only playing at one Art Theater on La Brea in Hollywood. Damn! Why couldn't it be at the Baronet instead of the 30th exploration of Fascist Italy? I knew Mom and Dad wouldn't let me borrow the car to see Jane Fonda's vagina on the big screen and besides, it was only playing "over the hill." So I convinced Lester Nafybal, who worked the album counter at Wallichs and was a *grown up* at 19, to take me in exchange for gas, dinner, and tickets.

Ohmygod!

A backyard swimming pool. It's night. Jane Fonda steps into view – nubile, spectacular, the perfect blend of innocence and sensuality.

Donned in a robe. I'm mesmerized. Even the annoying sitar music doesn't spoil the moment. And then…

As advertised… as anticipated… as prayed for—She removes her robe. I practically gasp. Jane Fonda is completely naked. On a diving board.

(*This* is why you snoop around Bel Air estates – not to see the damn Beatles!)

My grateful eyes never left the screen. If God can create a creature like Jane Fonda and in His divine mercy allow me to see her naked on a diving board, then He must truly exist. For several days after I walked with a swagger. Yes, I was still a virgin and no, that wasn't about to change anytime soon – but I was different, changed. I had become a man. I had seen a French movie!

There Goes My Career As a Mechanic

School resumed mid September. Half the girls returned that fall with new noses. This was the "sweet sixteen" birthday gift-of-choice. Boob jobs would come later when all the bat mitzvah savings bonds matured. But I must say, most of these girls did look considerably better sans Aunt Sadie's honker.

Due to overcrowding (everyone moved out to the suburbs – "build a mall, they will come"), Taft instituted an eleven period day. Classes were held from 7:00 AM till 5:00 PM to stagger start and stop times. Since I was an esteemed member of the varsity basketball team (with a big asterisk when it came time to wearing a letterman's sweater), I had an early schedule (allowing for afternoon basketball practice). Locker-mate Gary began his day at 11:00. But that meant he was able to swing by a local delicatessen and pick up corned beef sandwiches for lunch. No more *tuna surprise* at the cafeteria and our locker smelled like Kaplan's Deli.

(A year later there would be raids by narcotic officers and the drug sniffing dogs would excitedly make a beeline right to our locker first. There were several big drug busts at Taft over the next few years. I think by 1968 we lead the Valley in football, tennis, debate, and hash.)

My hours at Wallichs were adjusted to accommodate school. Tuesday and Thursday from 5:00-10:00 and Saturday 10:00-5:00. So on Tuesdays and Thursdays I didn't even begin homework until 11:00. Plus, this was the all-important *eleventh grade*. UCLA hung in the balance.

I was, by then, a declared Math major so in addition to History, English, and Spanish, I was taking Trigonometry and Calculus. I got very little sleep that year. You might say, "So why didn't you just quit your job?" And I'd say, "What? And give up show business?"

The one course that was a killer for me was Spanish. For some reason my mind just doesn't work that way. I was "muy stupido" if that's how you say it. I could only remember one phrase: "Luisa tienne catarro." *Luisa has a cold.* That's it. And I'm not even sure *that's* right. Vocabulary was impossible and worse still, was gender-specific grammar. I once got in trouble for asking if someone has a sex change operation would he/she have to go back and completely rewrite all their papers?

It did not help that my teacher was a complete buffoon. Mr. Valenzuela seemed to struggle with the language himself. And he grew up in Mexico! Plus, he clearly had a thing for the cute coeds. He saw himself as "Don Juan"; they saw him as "Cheech Marin." But all girls had to do to get an A on an oral exam was wear a tight sweater. Even Jody Lambert who had a cleft palate. I barely squeaked through that course with a C.

Mr. Fox in Trig was not a Dodger fan. He referred to me as "O'Malley lover!" (Walter O'Malley owned the team). When the Dodgers got into the World Series against Baltimore, Mr. Fox made me a bet. He could add up all of Baltimore's runs and they would still total more than all of the Dodger runs multiplied. I cheerfully took the bet, chuckling at what a sap he was. I had forgotten what a spectacular pitching staff the Orioles had. In game two the O's shut out the Dodgers 6-0. That meant that all the Dodger runs had to be multiplied by zero, which of course then totaled zero. Baltimore swept the Dodgers in four straight and I spent the rest of the term as Mr. Fox's little blackboard-cleaning bitch.

As a prelude to the SAT's, you took PSAT's (Practice Scholastic Aptitude Tests) in October. Today students enroll in courses and hire tutors to prepare for the SAT's, but back then you just showed up, took the exam, and got it over with. So after a particularly long Friday night ushering at the Valley Music Theater and convening at Bob's Big Boy with the other ushers to share our favorite moments of Earnest Borgnine trying to sing, I staggered into school at 8:00 AM on Saturday to take my PSAT.

When the results came back I ranked at the high end of cretin. Not only could I not get into UCLA with that score, I couldn't get into Wally Thor's Truckmaster School. But I wasn't worried. I knew if I knuckled down and got more than four hours sleep I would do fine on the SAT's. And I did. Not great but certainly good enough, which satisfied the high standard I always set for myself scholastically.

Now the *state* aptitude tests were a different story. These were a series of tests intended to determine which career path might be best for us. One test was *spatial relations*. We'd see a folded house and be given four flat layouts. Which layout, when folded properly would match the house? (Other than working for Ikea, how could this skill possibly help you? I think I finished in the 40th percentile.)

Worse was *mechanical reasoning*. "If Gear A turned left and Gear B turned right, how does a steam engine work?" I had no fucking idea how to answer any of these questions. I placed in the 25th percentile. That has to be in the severely retarded range, doesn't it? Lemmings score at least in the low 30's.

The only test I excelled at was *clerical proficiency*. As fast as we could we had to copy sequences of letters. I placed in the 78th percentile. So according to the State of California, my life's calling was filing.

Thanks to Miss Harper for uncovering another option.

Miss Harper taught U.S. History. Instead of tests she would assign us several essay questions on Monday that had to be turned in on Friday. To answer the questions you needed to digest her lectures and read the chapters. Essay writing has never been my strength. I would slog through the material and vomit back as much as I could. My grade was usually B-.

One week I put off the assignment until the last night. Having worked at Wallichs that evening, it was well after midnight before I tackled the essay. I didn't have time to do all the reading so I padded the paper with a few jokes. If I were going to fail at least I'd do it spectacularly.

I got an A.

Miss Harper put little exclamation points after the jokes (no one knew from LOL in those days). Finally! A woman recognized that I was funny! Now if I could just find one that was under 40. Still, it was my first real glimmer of validation.

The following week I sprinkled in a few more jokes.

Another A.

By week three, I had stopped reading the textbook entirely. I just used the essay topics as springboards and wrote comedy monologues. I suspect the quality of the material was not that stellar but I was Noel Coward compared to the twenty-five other explanations of the Monroe Doctrine.

I breezed through that course with an A and a light went off in my head – I might really be cut out for this comic essay stuff. What a relief because I knew alphabetizing was never going to win me Laura Petrie.

Thank you, Miss Harper, for being my first and maybe most important fan.

And the Hits Just Keep On Coming

Music was exploding in all different exciting directions in 1966. The Mamas & the Papas brought rich new harmonies. Little did we know that Papa John Phillips was sleeping with his daughter, McKenzie. And Mama Michelle was sleeping with Papa John and Papa Denny. And Papa Denny was sleeping with Mama Michelle and Mama Cass.

Brian Wilson and the Beach Boys were introducing innovative chord changes (quite a leap for the group that sang *"She makes me come alive/And makes me want to drive."*). "Winchester Cathedral" by the New Vaudeville Band sparked a whole nostalgia wave back to the '20s. And the Beatles blew everyone's mind with the release of their *Revolver* LP. It seemed with each new album they were taking giant leaps musically. In *Revolver* they experimented with new recording techniques, far more complex themes and arrangements, and laid the groundwork for their even more ambitious and groundbreaking albums to come. Many claimed that *Revolver* was the first psychedelic LP. But how would anyone know? Take enough drugs and "Turkey In the Straw" would sound psychedelic.

And then there was bubble gum, the Motown Sound, folk-rock, R&B, country soul, blue eyed soul, lady soul, regular soul. Garage bands, big bands, jug bands, English bands, Baja Marimba Bands. Even Sinatra. Hell, you had *two* Sinatras – Frank and his daughter Nancy. To my knowledge he never slept with her.

It Was a Very Goodyear

All you need to know about my dating life during this period is that I was thrown off the *Dating Game*.

The *Dating Game* was a popular afternoon game show on ABC where three bachelors vied to be selected for a date by (in theory at least) a beautiful bachelorette. She would be separated by a wall and unable to see the contestants. Her selection was based on answers to the inane questions she posed.

Buoyed by my comedic triumph in History Class, I decided to try out. "What the hell? At least this time if I'm rejected I get nice parting gifts." I called and got an invite to their monthly open audition. Now this meant driving "over the hill," but I figured it might be my last chance ever to date a lovely bachelorette so I sucked it up.

There must've been about fifty of us. First step was a brief interview with a production assistant. I confessed right up front that my father worked for ABC radio and if that were a conflict I'd just bow out. She said it was no problem. In fact, there had been emergency situations where even staff members had to fill in. I also said I was 16. No worries there either. From time to time they played the game with teens.

On to step two. They broke us into groups of ten and began asking us sample questions. It was fun and silly and I have no idea what I said, but I got laughs. This yuckmeister stuff was really starting to pay off!

The next day they called, inviting me to be a contestant. Cool! They said to wear a sports coat and "remember the show is in color." So for reasons that escape me, I went out and bought a GREEN jacket. I looked like I had just won the Master's.

The Dating Game was taped at ABC in Hollywood; the same ABC that housed *Shindig*. This time I managed to find it without veering off into riot country.

They taped several episodes at one time. I arrived late in the afternoon and was escorted into the bachelor's holding area. There were twelve of us – six for each episode. They all looked like Sean Penn… and wore blue or brown jackets. A production assistant briefed us. We would be escorted to the set for a walk-through – where to go if you won or you lost, where to stand, don't look directly into the camera, don't swear, etc. We did not see the lovely bachelorette ahead of time, nor did she see us. We were also not given a preview of the questions. Everything was very above board.

When my time arrived to play the game, as Bachelor #1 I was led into the studio during a commercial break. In the fleeting seconds before we were on the air I decided to revise my objective. The hell with the date! Be funny. Score for the studio and home audience. In an odd way that helped me relax. Yes, it's tough to be funny on demand but being *charming* was, for me, much tougher. Fortunately, she asked great moronic questions.

Bachelorette: "Bachelor number one (me), if I was a fruit, which fruit would you want me to be?"

Me: "An orange."

Bachelorette: "Why?"

Me: "So I could squeeze your navel."

Big laugh. Why I don't know. That was pretty stupid.

Bachelorette: "Bachelor number one, which would you rather take me to – a love-in, a drive-in, or a sit-in?

Me: "A drive-in."

Bachelorette: "Why?"

Me: "Because if I took you to a drive-in we could sit-in and love-in at the same time."

Another big laugh. Okay, that was a good one. And finally…

Bachelorette: "Bachelor number one, would you describe bachelor number two?"

Me: "A blimp."

Big laugh. Truth is he looked like Robert Redford, the son of a bitch.

Bachelorette: "Why?"

Me: (just being an asshole) "Because he has Goodyear written down the side of him."

That totally gratuitous cheap shot scored the biggest ovation of all.

It must've been rigged! I lost. Goodyear won.

The host, Jim Lange, introduced me. I walked around the partition and met her. Her look of relief was palpable—to me and probably America. Not that she was such a stunner. She was thin, scrawny, and just cried out *eating disorder*. The date was a yacht cruise around Newport Beach with the singing group the Turtles. Instead I got some nice Jantzen sweaters that I wore for years. And a thousand tubes of Gleem toothpaste.

Three weeks later the show aired. There were no VCR's (dinosaurs still roamed the earth back in 1966) so the only record of my appearance is a few slides my dad took off the television screen. Yikes. I had no business disparaging anyone's appearance. I looked like a stalk of broccoli with glasses. Oh well. It was only NATIONAL TELEVISION!!

But the next day I got a call from *The Dating Game* inviting me to be on their alumni show. And for weeks after that first episode aired, customers at Wallichs would recognize me as "that *guy*."

I don't remember my answers on the alumni show. At one point I vaguely recall imitating Elvis and saying my hobby was "skeet shooting with my rabbi."

I lost. Even with my spiffy *blue* sports jacket. This time the girl was gorgeous. And the lucky couple got to be the grand marshals of the Indio Date Festival. Instead, I came home with 25 pairs of Ray-Ban sunglasses. And a thousand more tubes of Gleem. I should run out in another eight years.

But then I got *the* call. The brass ring. The Holy Grail. I was invited on the nighttime version. Date destinations: Paris and Hawaii. I had never even been on a plane. Hand me that blue blazer. I'm going to war one more time!

So a few weeks later I returned to ABC and the process began again. Except this time, NABET (the engineer's union) was honoring an AFTRA radio talent strike (more on that later) so executives had to man the cameras. During my run-through one of the executive/cameramen recognized me and mentioned to someone that he worked with my father. We get back to the green room before the taping and I'm called out. I was off the show. What?! I reminded them of my initial interview. It made no difference. Show creator/ CIA spy Chuck Barris *himself* made the decision. They just grabbed someone from the audience wearing a jacket that wasn't green and stuck him in there. Had I won I would have gone to Barcelona. Needless to say, I was crushed.

But a few years later, when I was 19, I ran into host Jim Lange. He remembered me ("You're the 'Goodyear' guy!) and upon hearing my tale of woe placed a call to the show's producers. Sure enough I got a call from *The Dating Game.* Did I want to be on their alumni show? "Was this the nighttime version?" I asked. "No," they said. "Then go fuck yourselves!" I said and hung up the phone.

Kiss the Rubber Chicken

My actual dating life wasn't much better. I thought there was some promise with Helen Papadakis but that didn't turn out swimmingly. A good start though. I took her to see *Thunderball* and then to Bob's Big Boy. She let me put my arm around her during the underwater fight sequence. She ate a French fry off my plate (always a sign of intimacy). And at her front door – the BIG moment – she let me kiss her goodnight. It was not a big kiss mind you. Lips only. But it wasn't the handshake and "I had a really fun time, and please accept these hundred tubes of Gleem."

I was so confident, I called her for a second date on Monday. Usually I needed at least three weeknights to ramp up the courage. She accepted and all was right with the world.

But on date number two I met her father. These are always awkward encounters. They look at you like you're going to knock up their daughter, get her hooked on heroin, and coerce her into joining a cult. We *polite young men* are always assuring them that we wouldn't dream of touching their daughter (much less do any of the things we fantasize about while masturbating nightly to them), and we all want to be astronauts. Still, I sensed a dislike that went beyond mere suspicion and apprehension. I started getting the vibe of *Jew Hater*.

Helen and I were hitting it off though, so I chose to rationalize that he wasn't anti-Semitic, he just preferred suitors of any other religion in the world.

I took her to Eckberg's Steakhouse. This was maybe my favorite restaurant in the world. It was in an actual house on a side street off Ventura Blvd. in Woodland Hills. The living room had been converted to a dining room large enough for maybe six or seven tables. You could see into the kitchen where the stork-like Mr. Eckberg cooked the steaks. His dowdy wife was the waitress. All she would ever say was "ice box rolls" when she put a basket of them on your table.

They were both in their 70s, although who knows? They could have easily been in their 90s. They lived upstairs. Mr. Eckberg was a force of nature. He took your order, he cooked your steak, and all the while, cackled like an insane person. If a customer put a nickel into an old jukebox, the song "I'm Looking Over a Four Leaf Clover" would play. Mr. Eckberg would turn it up full blast and begin to dance and sing at the top of his lungs, all the while ringing dozens of bells. Helen thought this was a riot.

Mr. Eckberg would only take cash and when you paid at his antique register he would chortle, "Money, money, money!" ring a few bells, and make you kiss a rubber chicken.

No guy ever got laid bringing his date to Eckberg's Steakhouse but damn it was fun!

On date number three, I drove Helen home (arriving safely before the midnight curfew), kissed her goodnight, got back into Mom's 1960 Comet, turned on the ignition… and the car wouldn't start.

Shit! Probably a dead battery, but maybe I had flooded the engine. So I waited five minutes, tried again, and still nothing.

I went back to the house, tapped lightly on Helen's bedroom window, and told her I needed to use the phone to call the Auto Club. She let me in, but by now was wearing a bathrobe. Nothing sheer, just a big comfy terrycloth robe. I called the Automobile Club and we sat in the kitchen waiting for the tow truck. About five minutes later her dad entered the room and almost had a seizure. There was his precious daughter in a state of disrobe (actually a state *of* robe) with this...this... *red sea pedestrian*!!

I hastily explained, trying desperately not to use any Yiddish expressions. "My battery is dead," I said, and he snarled, "It better be!" With that he dashed out to the car and told me to start it up. I turned the key just praying it wouldn't start. Thankfully, it didn't. He stomped off to the garage and returned a moment later with jumper cables. In short order he got my engine to kick over. I thanked him profusely and he leaned into me and said, "Your fucking car is blocking my driveway."

O-kayyyy.

That was the last time I ever went out with Helen.

Improbable Victories

Ronald Reagan was running for governor. This seemed preposterous to me. He was an actor. Not even a good one. Over the last couple of years he was giving speeches on behalf of the Republican Party. He was a good speaker. Acting and public speaking are great qualifications for hosting the Oscars, but not necessarily for running the State of California. Yet, there he was, challenging popular incumbent Edwin "Pat" Brown. This was not unprecedented. One of our senators was George Murphy, another mediocre actor. *Those who can't do, govern.*

On Election Day in November the Taft basketball team was slated to play at Manual Arts. We all boarded the bus with great trepidation. This was a fluke in the schedule. We're used to playing teams in the West San Fernando Valley – sprawling campuses, excellent facilities, and… oh, let's just say it – white kids. Manual Arts was in the inner city. "The Big K Kingdom."

The gym was dark and foreboding. The stands were raised. The crowd looked down onto the court. Picture the arena in *Gladiator* with obscene graffiti. Our team came out to warm-up to a rousing chorus of boos. The Manual Arts team emerged. Ten Wilt Chamberlains only bigger.

This figured to be a slaughter. On the other hand, I'm sure Taft had the better golf team.

Miraculously we hung in there. And with two seconds to go, Mark Licht hit a fifteen-footer and we won. Coach Furlong gathered us all together and said, "Get on the bus. Just get on the bus. Shower back home. But right now, get on the goddamn bus!"

We beat a hasty retreat to the Safe Fernando Valley. And as if our win wasn't improbable enough, on the ride home we learned that Ronald Reagan would be our next governor. Bad times lay ahead.

The Return of Ann

The end of the year was a busy time. We hardly saw Dad. Rehearsals were nightly for the annual holiday Miline Club Show. He was very excited having won the plum role of Daisy Mae for that year's spoof of *Lil' Abner*. We were all so proud. I continued to juggle basketball, schoolwork, Wallichs, the Valley Music Theater, and the odd date (some more odd than others).

One day I was stunned when Michelle Rosenberg, a girl way out of my league, approached and actually spoke to me. She was taking a major risk. If the wrong people saw this she could be banished from her choice lunch area table. She further shocked me by saying there was a big upcoming dance just after Thanksgiving. Ohmygod! Was she actually asking ME to go with her?

No. Of course not.

They wanted a DJ to host it and she had heard I was a big radio geek. Could I get one? Hiding my disappointment, I said sure. She thanked me and started off. I called back, "Hey, can I have your number in case I need to reach you?" "Oh, I'll see you in school," she said and disappeared.

If nothing else, this task was a way to improve my popularity standing, which currently was below lepers and hall monitors. Securing one of these deejays was going to be tough. I didn't know any of the KHJ Boss Jocks. KFWB and KRLA were somewhat out of favor. But in the valley we had our own station, KBLA out of Burbank. Their signal was awful, they had no budget for contests, but it was kind of cool to have our own dinky local station.

One of their jocks was really catching on. Harvey Miller came from Philadelphia and changed his name to Humble Harve. He had a rich deep voice and came across as super hip. On Sunday nights he hosted "Stone City" – two straight hours of Rolling Stones music. And not just the hits – long album cuts. The fourteen-minute "Goin' Home" no less. Even FM stations weren't that daring yet. Humble Harve was becoming a sensation with us "Stoneagers," as he called us.

I sort of knew him. I had talked to him a couple of times on the request line. DJ's at KBLA always answered the request line unless they were just too stunned that someone was actually calling. So I dialed him up. He answered on the first ring. Seriously, no one listened to that station. Much to my delight and relief, Humble agreed to host the dance. He even recorded a promo to play on our school's P.A. system.

I had crossed the River Jordan. I thought, "I'm on my way." Party invites, cookouts at the beach, TP'ing houses, dating Michelle whose father had to not hate Jews (their last name was Rosenberg). My whole social world was about to improve.

And then came the night of the big dance. As I was waiting for Harve to arrive, someone else walked into the room.

Ann.

I almost plotzed. I hadn't seen her in a couple of years and the transformation was startling. She had gone from an adorable little 13-year-old to a positively stunning young woman of 16. I truly found it hard to speak. But she was still the same Ann – approachable and disarming. The power of speech slowly returned and I learned she still attended Catholic School and was there at the dance tagging along with a friend.

I was supposed to wait at the door for Harve, but they began playing a slow song. I asked her to dance. And once again in the middle of a brightly lit gymnasium I held Ann in my arms. I wanted those old feelings to return, I wanted to relive that euphoria I experienced the last time I danced with her. But I knew that was dangerous. Before, when I was 12, dancing close, her body pressed to mine; that was the be-all and end-all. Now I craved more. Now I longed to kiss her and explore her and even enter her. But I knew that would never happen. So why yearn for something I can never have? So I told myself, enjoy the dance then let her go. Which I did.

She went off with her friend. I went back to the door just as Harve arrived. That was shock number two.

Styles were changing. Everyone was growing their hair as long as legally allowed. Jeans and leather and suede were the off-campus rage – "Early Hippie." And Humble Harve took the stage... wearing a three-piece gray suit. There was a collective gasp. He could not have looked more square if he were Ronald Reagan.

Ann tapped me on the shoulder. She was going to leave. Yeah, her and everybody else. So much for my dreams of popularity. And Ann.

By 10:00 I was home watching *The Time Tunnel.* Every week, stars Tony and Doug were transported somewhere back in time. I envied them. This week they landed in the Spanish Inquisition. I still envied them.

As for Humble Harve, several months later he was hired away by KHJ and given a complete makeover. Flowered shirts, jeans, boots, and at all times, sunglasses. His new catchphrase was "spread love."

Unfortunately, his image as a cool mellow flower child would be somewhat tarnished when he shot his cheating wife to death a few years later. Talk about someone else who could have used a Time Tunnel.

Harve went to prison, got back into radio after his release (originally doing the mid-day "housewife" shift at a station, which I found amusing), and I know this sounds absurd in light of the events, but he is one of the nicest, gentlest souls I've ever met.

The Return of Dana

I worked my ass off Christmas vacation. Twelve-hour shifts at Wallichs, seven days a week. It was almost inhuman. Not the work; having to listen to goddamn Christmas music all friggin' day. Even now, if I'm at your house and you play Andy William "Little Drummer Boy" I *will* turn into Claudine Longet and shoot you.

The store was jammed-packed with customers during the holiday season. To discourage shoplifting, management hired a security officer to monitor the crowd. One day I noticed that Dana came in with a few of her mean girl friends. I went to the security officer and asked if he'd do me a favor.

A moment later, he approached Dana and asked to look inside her bag. He accused her of stealing a record. This caused quite a scene and Dana was thoroughly humiliated in front of all her friends and the fifty or sixty other customers in the store at the time. I then wandered over, "wondering" what all the commotion was about. The guard filled me in. I said, "Well, I know this girl and I'm sure there's been some mistake." He said, "Well, all right. If you'll write a note I can keep on file, I'll let her go and forget the whole thing." "A note?" I said. "You want me to write a *note* for Dana? Gee, that didn't work out too well the last time." Out of the corner of my eye

I could see her really squirming. "Okay," I said and scribbled down some note. He moved on. Dana thanked me. I couldn't have been more magnanimous. No, she didn't apologize for the incident two years before, but just embarrassing her and having her thank me for it was more than sufficient. (Would it surprise you to learn I later co-wrote all of the *Cheers* episodes where the bar got into an escalating practical joke war with rival Gary's Olde Town Tavern? Be careful whose heartfelt notes you pass around, girls.)

On December 15th Walt Disney died of lung cancer. He was 65. No generation took it harder than we did. Walt shrewdly surmised in the early '50s that television was the greatest marketing tool ever invented. Sing along Mouseketeers:

"M-I-C…see you real soon. K-E-Y … Why? Because we want to sell you merchandise, pimp our upcoming movies, and get you salivating over this new amusement park currently under construction. M-O-U-S-E."

We were the TV generation, dating back to the '50s. The daily afternoon Mickey Mouse Club was boomer catnip. We boys wore Davy Crockett coonskin caps. Our first crush was Mouseketeer Annette. And then in the mid '50s, Walt introduced us to a previously unimagined new world – a world of fantasy and excitement and wonder. Annette sprouted breasts.

So word of Uncle Walt's death hit us hard – an early reminder that life is not like Disneyland and you can wish upon all the stars you want, but if you have lung cancer, you're in deep shit.

My Hanukah gift that year was the best – a car. Okay, not a new one. Mom got that – a Chrysler 300 the size of a city bus. I got the 1960 Comet (now with new battery for when I date Klansmen's daughters). Freedom was mine!

Mr. Satisfy

Who you went out with on New Year's Eve was always a big deal. This was a special occasion. A girl couldn't go out with just "any Ken Levine." So Ken Levine never went out. Except now I had a car. There was no way I was spending the night in my room. And besides, KHJ would *send* you their list of the Big 93 hits of 1966. You didn't have to write them all down yourself – like some really pathetic loser whose name I won't mention did the previous year. My de facto sister, Terry didn't have a date either so we decided to go to a movie and dinner together.

We went to the Topanga Theater to see the latest Matt Helm film. Dean Martin as the secret agent whose blood alcohol level was 00.7. We followed that with dinner at a neighborhood Chinese restaurant, shared a platonic kiss at midnight, went to our respective homes and threw up for the next six hours, both victims of food poisoning.

Bring on 1967!

Historians claim 1967 was a year of growing polarization. The Hippies vs. the Establishment. Hawks vs. Doves. Long hair vs. short.

But *every* year was a year of polarization. Those merely joined the list of: Ringo vs. Me. Jocks vs. Me. Scholars vs. Me. Neil Young vs. Me.

My wardrobe was starting to change. I wore jeans (when I wasn't at school or at work, so four hours a week). I recall having a gold velour long sleeve shirt for some ungodly reason. Did I want to look like Captain Kirk? Add to the list: Me vs. Me.

The very first Super Bowl took place in Los Angeles in January. It didn't have a Roman numeral because no one was certain there'd be a Super Bowl II. It wasn't even called the Super Bowl. It was the AFL-NFL World Championship Game. Both CBS and NBC carried it. NBC had a snafu and didn't get out of commercials until after the second half had begun, so, if you can believe it, they halted play and started the second half over.

But it was blacked out in L.A. The 100,000-seat Coliseum missed selling out by only 40,000. Some blame the ticket prices. They were asking twelve whole dollars a seat! The Super Bowl is a major event today, but back then it was more of a novelty. The established NFL was far superior to the upstart AFL. David vs. Goliath's little sister. Together, both networks had a combined audience of 26.8 million. (In 2011, that total had risen to 100 million. But in fairness, we didn't have GoDaddy.com ads back then.)

The mighty Vince Lombardi-led Green Bay Packers easily defeated the Kansas City Chiefs 35-10.

But people in Southern California were pissed that access to the telecast was denied (which certainly contributed to that low viewer total. LA is kind of a big market.). There were articles in the paper showing how you could string wire hangers together and create antennas strong enough to receive the signal from San Diego. There were probably more deaths that year in Los Angeles from idiots falling off of roofs than car accidents.

I did get to see the game, however. We visited my grandfather, who was in the Veteran's Hospital in West Los Angeles, and somehow they were provided a feed. So me, my little brother, and fifty of the scariest old men you've ever seen in ratty blue bathrobes, on crutches, toting portable oxygen tanks, sat in the bleak dayroom and watched one black-and-white TV. I'm proud to say I attended the first ever Super Bowl Party. Me and the guys from the Spanish-American War.

I can also say I was the first person at Taft (or anywhere white people lived in the Valley) to discover Wolfman Jack. One night I was tuning around my radio looking for distant signals and came upon this eerie station from Mexico. The music was all hard R&B and Blues and the disc jockey had this macabre otherworldly voice drenched in echo. He called himself the Wolfman and was broadcasting on the "Big X" – XERB. His only sponsor was something called "Mr. Satisfy," a bottle of pills you could send away to Tijuana for that was guaranteed to give you guys "staying power" in the sack. This was quite a contrast to the Dippity-Do hair gel being hawked on KHJ. What I loved most about the Wolfman was how subversive he was, how utterly non-mainstream. A few years later he's starring in George Lucas movies, trading Muddy Waters songs for Bobby Vee oldies on a syndicated radio show, hosting network dance parties, and emceeing Halloween shows at Knott's "Scary" Farm.

Add to our list: The Deeply Committed vs. The Sell-Outs.

At least in the early part of 1967 the deeply committed were still holding strong though.

For the moment.

Eleanor, You're My Pride & Joy, et cetera

It was getting harder and harder to spend time with Gary. His afternoon part-time job became a full-time, seven-day-a-week job (and this on top of school). Gary worked for his father, who owned a company that made church annuals. So it's not like he could quit his dad. We'd still get together for lunch period, but burgers at Bob's Big Boy, going to Elvis and Anouk Aimee movies, or playing pool was now out. Only once can I remember him telling his father he absolutely had to have a Thursday night off. He saw that the Ike & Tina Turner Review was playing one-night-only at the Chatsworth Bowl.

I wasn't a huge Ike & Tina fan and figured, how good could anybody be if they were booked into a bowling alley? But it was a rare chance to hang out with Gary so I tagged along.

Ho-ly shit!

Tina Turner was the sexiest woman I had ever seen. I was like that wolf in the Looney Tunes cartoons with his tongue hanging out and his eyes flying out of his head as if they were on springs. Tina writhed, she growled, she slithered, and my teenage hormones exploded. I had never seen anything like this. The truth is I never found her particularly attractive (even that night), but the raw sexuality that just oozed out of every pore knocked me on my 17-year-old ass.

This was my second major sexual revelation. The first was seeing a young woman breast-feed her child in the waiting area of Stern's BBQ when I was thirteen. There it was – unleashed – an actual tit! Some people discover their sexuality on moonlight beaches or hilltops overlooking the twinkling lights of the city. I discovered mine in a bowling alley and rib joint.

I was left with an insatiable need to get a girlfriend. Actually, the need was to get laid but that couldn't happen *until* you were in a committed relationship for as many months as it took to doggedly wear her down.

I thought about maybe trying Helen again, but didn't want to risk having my house burned down by her father and the Cossacks.

My "sister" Terry was on the Drill Team. Like at most schools, Taft girls fell into one of three categories. The popular girls who had boyfriends to go with to football games, the unpopular girls who felt they had no shot and always stayed home, and then that group in the middle who didn't have boyfriends but were ever hopeful. These girls were called "the Drill Team." Several hundred of them would march in formation during halftime shows, twirling flags and making sharp left turns, hawking their wares. (Today we'd call them "e-Harmony members.")

So this was a rich vein of potential girlfriends to tap into and Terry was gracious enough to provide me with some introductions. The one I sparked to was Eleanor.

Eleanor was extremely cute. Huge blue eyes, a slight over-bite (which works for me), svelte figure, and a pre-Dorothy Hamill wedge haircut. She seemed perky and lively and based on Terry's recommendation, accepted a date with me.

I took her to see the Doors and Jefferson Airplane in concert at the Birmingham High football stadium. Both groups had a hit or two and this was that brief transition period between small clubs and giant venues. Now I'd like to say that the night was electric and I just knew I was witness to the start of a musical revolution, but actually the acoustics weren't great. Gracie Slick of the Airplane was amazing, but Jim Morrison of the Doors was on autopilot, and Eleanor didn't shut up during the entire concert.

During "Volunteers of America" she mentioned she was a witch, all through "Back Door Man" she discussed her childhood diseases, and as "Light My Fire" was building to a stirring crescendo she revealed her real passion was shoes.

Afterwards we went to Sambo's for dessert (yes, there was an actual coffee shop chain named "Sambo's"). Her months in bed with mono required no further details (although I would hear them again... and again... and again). I followed up on the witch thing. "So you mean you're like Samantha in *Bewitched*?" "No," she snorted, "that show is so unrealistic." (Really? You mean you *can't* wriggle your nose and turn someone into a gerbil? Why isn't there a disclaimer at the beginning of the show?)

It's been awhile so I hope I can recall this correctly. Jesus blessed her by making her beautiful, but with the extra attention came people who would take advantage of or resent her. And so, as protection, since He might find himself preoccupied with other things (like seeing that the Packers covered the spread in the Super Bowl), He also blessed her by making her a witch. Her faith in Jesus was rewarded with an interest in the occult. And she now had the power to inflict curses (which she assured me she only did when absolutely necessary). I think that's pretty much the gist. It was always my understanding that the Christian Bible strongly denounced any occult practices because they were the work of Satan, but why quibble?

She squeezed my hand as we walked to her front door and kissed me on the lips. Suddenly she went from major nutcase to delightfully eccentric.

Such are the concessions we make for a potential first girlfriend.

We started going out every Saturday night, usually to concerts. At the Teenage Fair ("over the hill" no less), we saw the West Coast Pop Art Experimental Band. This was a loud screechy psychedelic rock band that featured a continuous light show. Kaleidoscopic images would swirl around the venue (in this case, a tent) trying to create the illusion of a "righteous" acid trip. That's the rock band I should have joined. "What instrument do you play?" "The movie projector."

Eleanor really "dug" this group. The Doors and the Jefferson Airplane she ignored, but the West Coast Pop Art Experimental Band – that she thought was "far out," "groovy," "mind blowing," and "righteous."

Other slang expressions of the day: "bummer," "heavy," "go with the flow," "high" (not "hi"), "out of sight," and "oh wow." And there was some heated debate over "uptight." Many used it in a negative sense to describe someone who was tense, retractable, unwilling to "go with the flow." Yet, in Stevie Wonder's hit song "Uptight (Everything's Alright)" it's a positive, a synonym for "out of sight," which makes it almost as groovy as far out.

I took Eleanor to see the Association at the Valley Music Theater. I was a little concerned that when they sang "Cherish" I would yearn for Bev Fine, but Eleanor talked through the whole song so that wasn't a problem. (They weren't "mind blowing" like the West Coast Pop Art Experimental Band.) With Bev and Ann, and even

165

Dana, I had very strong feelings, but with Eleanor I just wanted to get into her pants. The notion of intimacy at that age, at least for me, was obliterated by physical desire. And to make matters worse, I was receiving no real gratification from either.

Eleanor was what we commonly called a D.D.H. – *damn door hugger*. I'm surprised she didn't fly out of the car whenever I took sharp turns (and there were a couple of nights I took sharp curves on purpose).

I would get my kiss on the lips goodnight. I would get to put my arm around her in the movies. And eventually we made out in my car. I was allowed to grope and pet but she always had to be fully clothed. I was never permitted to learn just how cold a witch's tit really is.

At school she was very friendly, but not particularly affectionate. If I held her hand she didn't pull away, but she never offered hers. She was usually surrounded by her magpie friends. Still, I would say we were an item… if only to the keenly observant.

I didn't fare much better with her at the Drive-In either. Drive-In theatres were big in the '60s. Gigantic parking lots with a huge movie screen. The novelty here was being able to watch movies in your car. In 1967, if someone opened a medical clinic where you could get gall bladder operations in your car, people would flock to it.

Usually B-movies were booked into Drive-Ins – cheesy horror flicks or Jerry Lewis comedies. No one cared. Everyone was groping and pawing in the back seat. I always thought it would be great if suddenly one night, that health film with Linda getting knocked up was shown.

Drive-Ins are highly romanticized, but I never really got it. The sound was always atrocious. You would attach these clunky portable metal speakers to the driver's side window. Everything sounded muffled and distorted. You were always going, "What did that mad professor say?"

There was usually one snack bar—a bunker that was a half-day ride on a bicycle from wherever you parked. Someone from your car would go to the snack bar and you'd see him again at the ten-year reunion.

The big attraction of course was privacy… well, semi-privacy. Kids could smoke dope or make-out unseen, except for all the lost souls walking by, tapping on your window, asking where the snack bar was. Eleanor was too self-conscious to let me do anything more than kiss her. Besides, she was very engrossed in the movie. How could you not be when *The Horrors of Spider Island* was unspooling?

The spring prom was coming up and I thought, okay, finally, here's the perfect time to really make my move. Rumor had it that lots of girls lost their virginity on prom night – it being a special occasion and more importantly, curfews were relaxed.

So I rented a tuxedo, bought her the obligatory wrist corsage, and escorted her to the elegant Taft multi-purpose room for this gala occasion. It was my first prom and I couldn't be more underwhelmed. Overdressed classmates awkwardly milling about drinking punch or standing in a long line to get their pictures taken. Missing *this* is what drove Janis Ian to madness?

After the prom I took Eleanor to Monty's Steak House in Encino for a nice dinner. You can't go to Shakey's in formal attire.

(Quick aside: Several years later there was a fire and Monty's burned to the ground. Everything was lost. Total rubble. Well… almost. Later it reopened in Woodland Hills and amazingly, *astoundingly*, all of the sports memorabilia (signed baseballs, Rams jerseys, etc.) made it unscathed. Nothing else. Just that. Can you imagine such… uh, *luck?*)

After dinner and admiring the sports memorabilia, we drove to a secluded spot up in the hills for a little *amore*. At first I stabbed myself on her corsage but things improved. We were making out, she was seemingly receptive so I reached behind to unzip her dress.

And she stopped me.

She wasn't ready to do that (at least with me). I lied and said all the right things – I really cared about her, respected her, she was the most beautiful girl in the entire world, I would pledge to a coven. No dice. But she said it was because of *her*, not me. And then she explained. I must say, I've been given the brush-off a fair amount in my life, but no rejection since Eleanor's could even *compare* when it comes to originality. She said she couldn't get involved because of her birthday. I said, "You have to be at least 16, you're a junior in high school." No, no. That's not what she meant. Her birth *date*.

Eleanor was born on June 15, 1950. That's the middle of the month, the middle of the year, the middle of the century. It was her lot in life to always be in the middle, always stay uncommitted.

Even at the time I thought, "Wow, that was impressive. She's a fucking loon but that was impressive."

We broke up after that. My birth date is February 14th. We weren't compatible. I was meant to gun down gangsters in a Chicago garage.

(Eleanor Epilogue: After graduation she was the first person in our class to get married. I guess numerology doesn't matter when the guy owns a motorcycle shop.)

So I was back on the market. Again.

Usually fix-ups can be awkward. Especially when the woman

who taught Sex Education sets you up with her daughter. Mrs. Richman, my Health teacher from last year, took me aside one day and suggested I take out her daughter, Becky. I had never met Becky. She went to Chatsworth High. Why Mrs. Richman thought *I* was the perfect match, I do not know. I'm guessing I was the safest guy she could find who wasn't gay.

So a blind date with a teacher's daughter – how could I resist? Much to my surprise and delight, Becky was beautiful. Big green eyes and a melt-your-heart smile. She was also very sweet. I was incredibly attracted to her, but every time I even thought of making a move, there was the vision of Mrs. Richman with her Gonorrhea handout. We stopped going out after a couple of dates – as if I could afford to be choosey. But it was just too weird.

This was the first time that I was the one breaking up. Usually it was the other way around. So of course, I was clumsy at it. I really didn't know what to say. Thinking back, I just cringe. Without going into particulars, let's just say I lied and said my birthday was June 15, 1950.

On the Line with Cliff Levine

AFTRA, the ABC radio talent union, went on strike that spring. (Remember my *Dating Game* trauma?) And NABET, the engineers' union, went out in support – at least on the radio side. That meant that KABC executives, in addition to their normal jobs, manned the control boards and became the air talent. My dad got tapped to do the morning sports and then host a talk show from 6:00-9:00 PM. So for about a month, until the strike was settled, he worked from 5:00 AM until 9:00 PM every weekday. And only regular days on weekends.

This is the infamous strike that cost me my trip to Barcelona when I got unceremoniously booted off *The Dating Game* without so much as a tube of Gleem toothpaste.

At first Dad just read the scores. But within a couple of weeks he was demanding the Lakers trade Rudy LaRusso and the Dodgers man-up and admit they were horseshit that year.

He began feeling more comfortable hosting the evening talk show too. It shocked him (and me as well) that callers were asking his opinion of Vietnam and the issues of the day. Why the hell did they care what he thought about anything? He was just some Joe

Schmoe. But because he was on the *radio*, they did. And then our neighbor would call constantly to badger him about trimming our hedge.

I must say it was kind of cool having my father be a minor celebrity. That was certainly new. Friends asked if it was weird hearing my dad on the radio. I'd say no, but every so often he'd voice an opinion or share some personal anecdote that I didn't know. *That* was bizarre. And then I wondered—what *else* is he revealing that I didn't know on nights I wasn't listening? Does Ruth in Downey and Lester from Alhambra know things about my father that I don't? I found this disconcerting but not so disconcerting that I'd listen to him over Vin Scully when the Dodgers were playing.

When the strike finally ended he said he was relieved. But deep down inside I think he missed it. In the end, he was better than some of the hosts he replaced.

The company may have given dad a bonus for his strike service because that spring we finally got a color TV! And just in time! ABC aired a documentary called "the Mini-Skirt Rebellion" in full color. It was a special report that took a closer look at this new fashion trend (short SHORT skirts) and what its impact on society might be. I imagine ABC pulled some reporters off the Arab-Israeli War to give this topic the extensive coverage it deserved.

For Jews everywhere that war was the greatest. The Arab states of Egypt, Jordan, Syria, Iraq, Saudi Arabia, Sudan, Tunisia, Morocco and Algeria went to war against Israel, and it took the tiny country only six days to defeat them all. As a result, Israel gained control of the Sinai Peninsula, the Gaza Strip, the West Bank, East Jerusalem, and the Golan Heights. The ramifications of that action proved far more significant than mini-skirts, but between the two revolutions, things were really looking up for me. Dresses were getting skimpier and Jews were becoming badass.

On a personal level, I sort of fantasized one day I'd see Helen in a mini-skirt and it would so excite me that I'd beat the crap out of her dad, take his daughter, and some of his yard.

Vote For Me... Or Not

In an effort to possibly impress more girls with my dazzling talent, I joined the staff of the school newspaper, the heralded *Taft Tribune*. Women swooned over guys who could draw pen-and-ink cartoons, right?

Apparently I was mis-informed.

My tenure at the *Trib* lasted three weeks. I asked the teacher, Mr. Rosen, if I could write something – maybe a sports piece or humorous column. "Nah," he said, "You're the *cartoonist*. Stick to that." So I did. But not for him. I quit the paper.

I can honestly say I became a writer *despite* the Taft English Department. That semester I got all A's except for one B. That was in English where Miss Swanly said I lacked writing skills.

Where I seemed to excel was in Math. And Math proved to be a very helpful tool in my comedy-writing career. How, you say? Math teaches you logic and when you plot out stories, that's all you're doing. Getting from scene A to B to C to D is the same process as solving equations.

I took the SAT test that winter and unlike the PSAT, I got a good night's sleep beforehand and really took it seriously. No one studied for the SAT's. Not in my high school at least. Yet we were competing with New York students who had the benefit of Leo S. Kaplan's tutoring service.

I'm sure I could have used some helpful tips, but my SAT scores were light-years better than my PSAT results. Certainly good enough to get into a decent university. I applied to UCLA (duh!), Cal Berkeley, Cal State Northridge, and Stanford. I wouldn't hear till the end of the year.

Now all I had to do was keep my grades up and run for Senior President.

My college advisor said that admission boards really looked favorably on students who showed initiative. School politics garnered the most bonus points. My only problem though, was that I didn't give a shit about school politics. The thought of being on stupid committees to look into pep rally budgets and new bylaws for hall passes bored the holy crap out of me. And I still hadn't fully recovered from that devastating defeat in Junior High.

But then I had a brainstorm. There was a growing mood of rebellion in the country. Not to where we were burning banks yet, but young people were beginning to assert their independence, speak out against perceived injustices like the Vietnam War and race relations, and reject the "system" they felt was outdated and just driven by money. Our parents' values were being challenged. The American Dream of owning a house and car and washing machine now felt superficial, materialistic, and "plastic."

To be one hundred percent honest, there was less of that at Taft because we *liked* our cars and disposable incomes and nice homes. And yes, there was the draft, but that was still several years off for *us* and besides, all we had to do to avoid it was go to college, and parents with means came in real handy when tuition bills came due.

But that's not to say we didn't sit around someone's pool and bitch about the bourgeois middle class.

And we were militant extremists compared to the kids at Webster Groves High School in Missouri.

CBS aired a one-hour primetime documentary called *16 in Webster Groves*. It was narrated by Charles Kuralt so you know they meant business. CBS selected the upper middle-class town of Webster Groves (an idyllic suburb of St. Louis) to examine the behavior and views of "typical" 16-year-old teenagers.

I watched the show, curious as to how similar their experience was to mine. Especially since their community sounded just like Woodland Hills except they had snow and we had Jews.

Wow! Talk about conformity – one girl was on camera saying, "Silverware makes you feel good. If you have silver to put on the table it does so much for you." Another had already picked out the house she wanted to live in for the rest of her life. It was across the street.

This was Stepford.

A big emphasis was placed on the pressure these kids felt to get good grades in preparation for college. And yet, they must've slept through history and poli sci since 99% of them knew who Dick Van Dyke was but only 20% were familiar with Ho Chi Minh, the communist leader of North Vietnam. (I wonder how many knew who Alan Ladd was.)

The kids were given an extensive survey prepared by the University of Chicago. They answered anonymously. The results were somewhat startling.

93% were concerned about the way they looked. (I think that number is a little low.)

Fewer than 25% thought heavy petting and making out was acceptable, even among couples going steady. (Huh?)

And here's the shocker – 96% rejected the idea of sexual intercourse, even at their age. (That can't POSSIBLY be true! Certainly not if *boys* took that survey. And probably a lot of the girls didn't feel that way either.)

This was a sea change for me. I was finally beginning to realize that despite Eleanor, girls craved sex too. What kept them from engaging in it was the magnitude and significance of the act. It had to be with someone super special. The emotional implications were enormous. And daunting. Too daunting in most cases. Oh. And then there was the minor issue of unwanted pregnancies.

But I knew enough to know that survey was bullshit. Even with Charles Kuralt narrating. There was hope! I just had to find the *right* girl. Oh, if only it was as easy as buying them nice silverware.

Anyway, my idea for beefing up my college application was this: Embracing this spirit of rebellion, I ran for Senior President on a platform that I would do nothing. I would abolish all committees; I would cancel all stupid senior events. And the beauty of this campaign was I didn't have to do a thing. No posters, no buttons, no big speech at assembly. Those all went against my platform. I was actually required to give a speech so I just walked to the microphone said, "Vote for me," and sat back down.

Yes, it was a goof but all university admission boards would see was that I ran for Senior President, so I must be a *caring, concerned, selfless individual with oodles of initiative.* So what if nobody voted for me? The last thing I wanted was to become Senior President for godsakes.

I did lose.

By sixteen votes.

Holy shit! I'll never make that mistake again.

You'd think my stunt and its unexpected acceptance would result in my becoming more popular. Nope. Just the opposite. The popular kids felt I was mocking them and resented it. So they continued to shun me. But now at least they knew just *whom*they were shunning.

But the use of humor, the device of pulling a prank, was to become the preferred method of getting attention by the new emerging political leaders. Jerry Rubin, Abbie Hoffman, and Paul Krasner were three activists who started the Youth International Party… or *Yippies*. They found that theatrics got them a lot more media attention than irate speeches on college quads. By shining a light on all the craziness, they made their point in a slightly less threatening way. So I like to think that I was one of the pioneers of this new protest movement. And the October 21st march on Washington when hippies tried to exorcize and levitate the Pentagon, you can trace the roots back to the senior presidential election at Taft High. You're welcome, counterculture.

Don't Drink and Watch Plays

L ike all teenagers (except at Webster Groves, according to their survey), I did my share of drinking. Drinking made you cool, drinking made you high, and drinking helped you *forget that broad, that dame, that "Angel Face" who broke your heart and mailed it to her mother.* (Okay, I listened to too many Sinatra albums.) But it was not uncommon on those not-so-rare weekend nights when I was dateless to rendezvous with a few other losers, each steal a beer or two from our respective fridges, and get together either at a Drive-In or the Bob's Big Boy parking lot to drown our sorrows and get shit-faced. I rarely got so blotto that I vomited on the carhop girls, but it wouldn't take more than two beers to propose to one of them.

There's one alcohol-related incident in particular that, to this day, I am appalled by. One Saturday when Gary's parents were out of town, he and I had a few brewskies over at his place. As a class assignment I was required to see the school play that night. So Gary and I shuffled off to Taft, and (it still pains me to write this) fifteen minutes into the play, something struck us funny, and we both went into uncontrollable hysterics. The laughing jag of all laughing jags. Here's the horrible part: the play was *the Diary of*

Anne Frank. At least we knew enough to not laugh out loud, but can you imagine? As Nazis were going through her house, the two of us were convulsing. I went home that night and knew I had to cool it.

And then came *Black Saturday.*

Six months later. I showed up at Wallichs a little before 10:00 to begin my shift. I was working the album counter with John Kerns. John was a great guy – recently graduated from college, and had that "who gives a shit?" aura that employers hate but fellow employees admired.

10:00 rolled around and John still hadn't shown. That was odd. He was always very punctual. At 11:00 we started to get concerned. The manager called his apartment and received no answer. Very curious. You see where this is going, don't you?

At noon the mystery was solved. John would not be coming in. Ever. At 4:00 that morning, completely intoxicated, John drove up an off-ramp onto the 405 Freeway. Going 80 miles-an-hour on the wrong side, he had a violent head-on collision with another car, killing him and the other driver instantly. Grizzly photos were in the next day's *Times.* Needless to say, it shook me up. My alcohol consumption went way way down. There won't be any stories of wild nights getting smashed, and wreaking havoc, and waking up in Flagstaff married to a carhop. Anne Frank and John Kerns – the two best reasons to drink responsibly.

Flower Power!

That was the slogan of the spring. It began in Berkeley as a symbolic gesture to protest our involvement in Vietnam.

The tide was beginning to turn with regards to that *crazy Asian War*. There seemed to be little progress, the troop build-up just kept swelling, and for the first time ever, Americans could watch the graphic images of war every night on television. (And that coverage was positively primitive compared to the live satellite feeds we receive today, not to mention blogs and Tweets from the front.) Back then, network correspondents filed two/three minute filmed reports that had to be shipped halfway across the world. And even though we saw these reports several days after the fact, they still packed a wallop. Every night we witnessed the confusion and carnage right there in our cozy living rooms. This was no John Wayne movie. This was real… with no end in sight. The nation as a whole, still pretty much pro-war, was beginning to have creeping doubts. You could sense that growing dissatisfaction among the callers who were "On the Line With Cliff Levine" every night on KABC radio.

So flowers represented peace and beauty and non-violence. Protesters were encouraged to hand flowers to soldiers, and policemen, and politicians, and spectators. A whole movement arose and "Flower Children" spread love and joy (and hay fever) throughout the land.

Some of us began to wear flowers in our hair. Yes, even me. That was a first – one of two firsts actually.

I took Lynette Berman to a Love-In at Reseda Park. These were becoming quite popular. Young people would gather at a park and usually a live band or two would perform. It was a very cool scene. Think of a giant picnic where everyone brought pot instead of potato salad. You basically fed off the positive energy of being with so many of your peers. And unlike high school gatherings, everyone here was equal. The popular kids didn't get to sit closer to the band. I could be skinny and wear glasses and not feel bad about myself. *Far out, man!* And if parking wasn't such a bitch I probably would have gone to all of these Love-Ins. Griffith Park, Elysian Park, and Silverlake hosted them too.

The granddaddy of Love-Ins was the Monterrey Pop Festival way up the coast. It was the forerunner for giant concerts that would culminate in Woodstock two years later. There's no way I could go. It was June. I had finals. And you talk about "over the hill," Monterrey was 350 miles away – that's over *fifty* hills! But I sure wanted to be there. The line-up was incredible. The Mamas and Papas (my then-favorite group), Otis Redding, the Who, guitarist Jimi Hendrix, and some blues singer named Janis Joplin. Today the Monterrey Pop Festival is a legend (to those old enough to have heard of it). but back then it was just another concert you'd see an ad for or hear about in passing on the radio. Only later was it considered a big deal. Still, of all the mega music festivals I missed – Woodstock included – *that's* the one I regret missing the most.

But getting back to Reseda, KBLA, our valley station, had been promoting the local Love-In. I overheard Lynette talking about it with friends and figured this was the perfect excuse to ask her out.

I was right. She accepted. One has to be resourceful when dating cute brunettes out of one's league. One also has to work one's ass off keeping the conversation going when one's cute brunette turns out to be a slug.

"So who's your favorite group, Lynette?"

"I dunno."

"I hear the Beatles have a new album coming out."

"Uh huh.

"Do you like the Beatles?"

"I guess."

"They're really experimenting with different sounds."

"I guess."

It was like playing tennis against a blanket.

The park was packed. The group was the Black Sheep, a local band that appeared to be on the verge of stardom. (It never happened. Maybe their problem was they didn't have a member who went to Taft. Steppenwolf, the Strawberry Alarm Clock, the Electric Prunes, Smith, and the Rose Garden all had current or former Taft Toreadors in their groups and all broke through to enjoy at least one Top 40 hit. And me with my idiotic harmonica.)

Some urchin was handing out flowers. Lynette took one and put it in her hair. I did the same. Proud to say I went a whole minute before feeling self-conscious and stupid. Yes, this was a non-judgmental, all-accepting environment but 5,000 years of genetic wiring told me I didn't look groovy; I looked like a Shriner at a convention luau.

Here's what else the well-dressed hippie was wearing in 1967: necklaces of silver and colored beads for men, hair bands (hair was getting decidedly longer), knee high leather boots (mostly for women but really, all bets were off), rawhide cowboy jackets for guys, Indian saris for women (anything American Indian, peace pipes in particular were popular), long flowing robes (primarily for women), Benjamin Franklin glasses (blame John Lennon for that one), bead string earrings, and for reasons that I never understood – bells for ankles and wrists. Realize, of course, that all us high schoolers on Monday morning had to go back to collared shirts, slacks, and dresses.

People were passing around joints. One finally came my way. I had never indulged. But Lynette took a hit and despite how "Jimmy" became a worthless bindle stiff from merely one puff, my curiosity was just too great, and I had to try it.

Within minutes I was hooked. By the end of the day I had graduated to crack, went through every dime I ever owned, and desperately began robbing people, even my own family, to feed my habit. Damn! Those films were *right*!

Uh... no.

I felt a little mellow, that's all. And to be honest, I'm not sure if it was the effect of the marijuana or just projecting how I was *supposed* to feel. I was a little more relaxed... but hardly what you'd call "stoned." I'd categorize it as a good enough feeling that I'd be willing to smoke more, but not good enough that I'd be willing to pay for it myself.

Still, I drove home that day proud of myself. I had the courage to try something potentially scary and dangerous (at least to me). But I walked in the house and there were my parents, giving me an odd look. Uh oh. They *knew*! They smelled it on my breath! Shit!

After an excruciatingly awkward pause they looked at each other and finally my father spoke. "What are you doing with that stupid flower in your hair?"

Thanks for signing my yearbook

1967 was the "*Summer of Love*," an event that began with the Monterrey Pop Festival or the Israeli War, depending on who you talk to. I wrapped up the semester with good enough grades to keep me in the UCLA derby. School annuals were distributed and passed around for comments. I can't make out half of them. And people who claim we'll be friends forever, I have no idea who they are. But here are a few semi-legible ones.

Ken
Glad you were not in any of my classes.
—Diane

Ken
Good luck and stuff and remember there's pot at the end of the rainbow.
—Steve S.

Ken
You're funny you flower child.
— Lynette

Mr. L,
You made me wait in line at Wallichs. I hate you.
– Jeff

Ken,
I wish you had become Sr. A Pres. You have the class to do it. Yet you lack those characteristics it takes to be one. 1) conceit 2)lack of ability. Therefore it could never happen. Kid you got my support always.
–Cecily

Kenny baby,
You got a great sense of humor and maybe someday you'll be funny.
–Larry

Ken,
You have many possibilities for the future. You would probably make a good comic writer for Mad Mag.
–Randy

Ken,
You are 1 of the most unusual people I know. Have a great summer.
–Pam

To Mr. Wonderful,
I enjoyed our little lunch lectures and all your side comments. Have a happy.
–Gary

God knows what I wrote in any of *their* yearbooks.

Poor Howard Halpren. His girlfriend, Ester Loeb wrote this in his yearbook:

Howard,
I know you want something more from our friendship but I'm not the
girl you're looking for. With the summer coming it's probably best that
we part – still friends of course but I don't want to go further at this
time. Don't be sad. I know you'll be OK. You have many fine qualities
and I know you will find someone else. That's what summers are for.
Be good.
–Ester

Yikes! Who breaks up with someone in their yearbook? Dana had
to put her up to it.

Love & Haight

The summer began with a family vacation. These were very rare. Non-existent almost. Back in the early '60s when dad worked at KRKD, he would trade commercial time for free trips to the Riviera Hotel in Las Vegas – the perfect destination for a twelve-year-old and an eight-year-old. But we loved it. We sat out at the pool all day long. It was 358 degrees but what did we care? We could just sign for everything. It's like the Rat Pack except we ordered ice cream sundaes instead of scotch.

By 1967, I had been as far south as San Diego, far north as Santa Barbara, far east as Las Vegas, and far west as the end of the Santa Monica pier. But that was about to change. My dad announced that we were going up to San Francisco.

Oh. My. God.

I had wanted to go to San Francisco more than anyplace else in the world. I was intrigued by all the buzz about the music scene there, Haight-Ashbury, *the Summer of Love*, and okay, I'll be honest – I just wanted to see a Giants game at Candlestick Park.

As always, we drove. I still had not been inside an airplane. Our family trips tended to be on the frugal side. We stayed at a Travelodge motel on Lombard St. in the Marina district. We should have slept in the Impala. It had more room.

But I didn't care. I was just thrilled to finally be there. We saw the sights, crossed the bridges, dined at Kans in Chinatown, hopped cable cars, slurped crab cocktails at Fisherman's Wharf, and gawked at the basketball-sized bazooms on Carol Doda, whose image was proudly and prominently displayed at the topless Condor club in North Beach, where she jiggled them three times nightly.

(Side note: Carol had risen to prominence in 1964 when many delegates from the Republican National Convention went to see her act.)

Candlestick Park was even colder and more miserable than advertised. It was situated in maybe the worst location for an outdoor sports facility EVER. Right on the bay in a wind tunnel. And Richard Nixon threw out the very first pitch. My guess is he split after the second inning and made a beeline to the Condor Club.

The next day I got my first glimpse of the Haight-Ashbury district. This was hippie Mecca, the epicenter of the counter-culture revolution. Love was free and the drugs were reasonable. With Scott MacKenzie's "San Francisco" as their anthem, young people from all over the country migrated to the Haight. Harvard Professor Dr. Timothy Leary, the noted advocate of psychedelic drug research (LSD), coined the catchphrase: "*Turn on, tune in, drop out.*" (That same year Leary would marry his third wife. Hard to tell if the bride was really beautiful that day; all the guests were on acid.)

This was a utopian society, an oasis where you were free of the shackles of expectation and civilization. A haven for spiritual awakenings, creative inspiration, and yes, even consciousness expanding. Forget that LSD was officially banned in 1967.

(Years later, Leary did a guest spot on an episode of *Frasier* playing a caller to Frasier's radio show. I co-wrote it. Yes, I can say I wrote comedy for Dr. Timothy Leary.)

Haight-Ashbury looked exactly as you've seen it in documentaries and movies of the '60s. Loads of hippies in colorful garb (some with face paint) milling about, rolling joints, playing guitars and tambourines. Murals on the sides of buildings, head stores and mom & pop markets. Vivid kaleidoscopic color everywhere – from tie-dyed clothes to rainbow store signs to a blue building with a yellow door. Imagine Jimi Hendrix as the art director of *Sesame Street*. But it was festive and fun.

And as we drove through this idyllic world I thought to myself, "Ugggh! How the hell can anyone live here? It's so dirty and crowded. What happens if you get sick? What kind of privacy would you have in one of these cramped apartments? How clean are the bathrooms? What's the TV reception like? Shouldn't those dogs be curbed?"

I had zero desire to *turn, tune, drop*, or whatever else was necessary to move to Haight-Ashbury and join this freaky scene.

It's one thing to be a hippie. It's another to give up creature comforts.

And I never took LSD, dropped acid, snorted mushrooms, or smoked bananas. I was too afraid of bad trips. People were using mind-expanding drugs for self-discovery. That's okay. I didn't need to know who I was that badly.

Hippies, by the way, never referred to themselves as *hippies*. They were *heads* or *freaks*. This misidentification is why they should have had business cards.

Every '60s -era movie contains the same plot. Clean-cut kid from Webster Groves is mesmerized by his first sight of Haight-Ashbury and goes down an Alice rabbit hole of drugs and sex and bad gurus. The truth is, 99.999% of the teen population did *not* relocate to San Francisco, and most of the kids who did were not homecoming kings and queens; they were troubled runaways. The Haight soon became a tourist attraction and drug use started taking its toll. There was growing disillusionment, a steep rise in crime, and rats. Everyone was still wearing flowers in their hair. But the bloom was definitely off the rose.

Still, I was glad to have seen it first-hand. At a time when young people are trying to discover just who they are, it was nice for me to realize just who I *wasn't*.

A full-time job awaited my return at Wallich's. I was promoted to stock manager. The previous stock manager, Alvin, had gotten drunk and exposed himself to some kids in the Market Basket parking lot. This may have been "*the Summer of Love*," but for me it was "*the Summer of Work*."

It was my responsibility to order and keep track of the inventory. All of the albums were in the back. Only the listening demos were in the store bins. So my stock room was essentially a giant library, categorized by label and record number. In the fall I'd be shifted to the album counter, which was the plum job because you got commissions. By then I'd know the inventory so well that someone would ask for an album and while the other salesmen were fumbling around, looking it up, I dashed back and produced it in a flash.

Late in June a ton of boxes from Capital Records arrived. Inside was the new Beatles album – *Sgt. Pepper's Lonely Hearts Club Band*. Hurriedly, we put it on in the store and I was completely knocked out by it. So innovative and original and groundbreaking. It's hard to believe how much they had grown as musicians. Just three years ago they were singing, "She Loves You/ Yeah Yeah Yeah" and now they're doing "Day in the Life" complete with its complex arrangement, full orchestra, and audio effects never before heard. Music historians will tell you this was the album that defined psychedelic rock and maybe the decade itself. All I know is this: we played *Sgt. Pepper's* continuously that summer. Nothing else. Just *Sgt. Pepper's*. I must've heard it 500 times that summer, maybe a thousand.

And I never got tired of it.

Still to this day, I could listen to *Sgt. Pepper's* on a continuous loop. I can't say that about any other album I've ever heard.

Sgt. Pepper also generated a fair amount of controversy because of its lyrics. There was much speculation that there were drug references hidden in them; "Lucy in the Sky with Diamonds" – LSD being the most obvious. Drug reference lyrics became the rage in this period. The Jefferson Airplane's "White Rabbit," Jimi Hendrix's "Purple Haze" are just two of many examples. Donovan made a career out of stringing non-sequiturs together that people interpreted as deeply meaningful.

Electrical bananas are sure to be the very next phase.

And I got expelled for "Ken Satisfies Best." I wonder if these rock poets realized that they weren't the first to slip drug mentions in song lyrics. Jazz musicians had been doing it since the '30s. And of course the lyric *I get no kick from cocaine* came from the world's very first hippie – Cole Porter.

But getting back to *Sgt. Pepper*, usually we'd get an initial rush when a highly anticipated album was released, but that would die down in a week. Not so with this one. Even though Montgomery Ward's—50-feet away—was selling it for two dollars less, we were moving hundreds of albums a day. *Sgt. Pepper's* topped the U.S. charts for a staggering fifteen weeks in a row. And yet, it wasn't the top selling album of the year.

More of the Monkees was.

One of my goals that summer was to put on weight. I was still a svelte 135 pounds. So I went on a program of Nutrament. This was a popular liquid diet supplement of the day. Each can contained 315 calories. So to *gain* weight you drank it along *with* meals. And in the afternoon. And at night. In theory it tasted like a malted. In reality it tasted like chalk. And not even good chalk. After a week of this, my stomach was reeling. After two weeks I had *lost* four pounds. So much for that experiment. I'm not sure if Nutrament still exists, but certainly a version is now what they use to clean you out before a colonoscopy.

One day, Ramona came into the store. I hadn't seen her in awhile. Ramona was the official class slut. She's the one who slept with, among others, her brother (I learned years later). I did a double take when I saw her. Ramona was eight months pregnant. This was the first time I had seen a classmate, someone my own age, "with child." (Yeah, like you, I'm wondering the same thing.) But it was more than a gentle reminder that I was approaching adulthood, at least biologically. Whether I wanted to or not, whether I was ready to or not.

The Semester of Rachel Salberg

Urban unrest and violence continued to rock the country. Angry rioters who practically burned down the cities of Detroit and Boston didn't get the memo about the *"Summer of Love."* In September, Former Alabama Governor, George Wallace spelled out how *he* would solve the problem. "Bam, shoot 'em dead on the spot! Shoot to kill if anyone throws a rock at a policeman or throws a Molotov cocktail. Don't shoot any children; just shoot that adult standing *beside* the kid that throws the rock." *Four terms* the people of Alabama elected this idiot. And in 1964, he made a serious run for president.

I returned to school that fall, skinny as ever, worried that I wouldn't be able to retain any European History or Calculus because I had permanently memorized the entire Warner Brothers Records catalog. Luckily that wasn't the case… most of the time.

But grades be damned. That time frame will always be fondly remembered as the *Semester of Rachel Salberg.*

I first met Rachel Salberg a year earlier when she was sitting in front of me in English Lit and the first day of class whirled around and said, "Hi, I'm Rachel." It took me by surprise. I wasn't used to girls being that forward – at least to me. So we became school chums. Rachel was a cute brunette but for whatever reason I never asked her out. Sometimes you place people in categories and that's the only way you see them. Terry was in the "sister" bin. Rachel was in the "friend" bin.

But this year she caught my eye. I don't know why, but I do recall thinking, "You are such a schmuck! She's adorable! How could you not see this for an entire year?"

So I asked Rachel out and she said yes. That Saturday night I took her to the Fallbrook Theater to see Woody Allen's *What's New Pussycat?* I didn't realize it was a bawdy sex farce. I found it hilarious but squirmed a little because the subject matter was so racy. (Well, racy for the times. Today you could probably show it uncut on the Disney Channel.)

After the movie we went next door to Nibbler's for pie. Being friends beforehand helped break the ice. I already knew she was Jewish and quite observant and that she liked to dance. What I didn't know was that her part-time job was teaching Hebrew at a local temple. "Oh my God!" I thought, "Here's this sweet girl, a Hebrew school teacher yet – and I take her to a PORNO MOVIE!" I figured I had blown it big time. But she seemed unfazed and gave me a goodnight kiss at her door that could almost be labeled *encouraging*. So much so that I boldly asked her out again – right there. And she accepted! Success to the sexual deviant!

The yearlong friendship really helped accelerate things because by the end of date two we were making out in my car. And unlike Eleanor, Rachel seemed to actually be enjoying it. (I could sense that Eleanor was on autopilot, but I had worked so hard to get to that point that I wasn't about to let a little thing like her disinterest get in the way.)

I called Rachel the next day just to thank her for a lovely evening and we stayed on the phone for an hour. Wow. That was new. The thought occurred to me – this was really bordering on *boyfriend/girlfriend country*.

In school we started hanging out together, even having lunch every day (Gary had graduated in June, that bastard). For 2 1/2 years I'd see happy couples walking hand-in-hand to the hash line and now I was one of them! I had a real girlfriend (not a whack-job like Eleanor). And the best part was this: it wasn't just the "concept" of being in a relationship that I found so intoxicating, or the desire for carnal gratification – it was Rachel. I was really falling hard for Rachel. *Love at first anniversary of first sight.*

I even declared my love for her… sort of. I took Rachel "over the hill" to Westwood to see the very popular French film, *A Man And A Woman*. As we're driving home I said to Rachel, "The ad says '*See this movie with someone you love*' so I guess I love you." She laughed, not taking me seriously. I kept the ticket stub – I *was* serious.

What I Did For the Slim Hope of Sex

This was my happiest time in high school. What a difference not being snubbed or ignored makes! I was living the *Big Man On Campus* dream – mighty senior, cool chick by my side, and fifteen disposable dollars every week just burning a hole in my pocket.

And Eleanor gave us her blessing. That was awkward. Rachel and I were sitting in the senior quad sharing a tuna sandwich one crisp autumn day when Eleanor approached. She said she had seen us together on campus a lot and thought we made a cute couple. She approved. With that, she flitted off. Rachel had had a few classes with Eleanor and thought she was really strange but still, what the hell was that all about? I sheepishly confessed that we had dated for a few months. "Really?" she said, scrunching up her face. "Yes," I replied, "But the good news is if *you* ever turn out to be completely bonkers I'll stay with you longer than I should." She laughed and that was that. But over the next few months, every time we'd pass Eleanor in the halls Rachel would turn to me and say something like, "So 'crazy' is your type, huh?"

We started going out both Friday and Saturday nights. And our make out sessions in my Mustang were getting longer. Finding a deserted place to park was always a challenge. The most popular spot was Mullholland Drive overlooking the valley but (a) it was crowded, and (b) policemen would skulk around and shine flashlights in your window. I didn't need Rachel screaming hysterically so I avoided Mullholland Drive. Instead, I discovered the Hughes Junior High parking lot. It was always empty and out of view from passing squad cars.

Unfortunately, our romantic interludes were not as lewd as I had hoped. We would French kiss and grope, but Rachel wanted to take it a little slow beyond that. After all, Rachel was a "good girl" and in 1967 they still had those. So it was somewhat frustrating, but honestly, I was delighted to be getting *this* far.

And week-by-week we were moving forward. Baby steps but progress nonetheless. By the Thanksgiving break she let me remove her bra. I was overjoyed until I tried to actually do it. I had never taken off a bra; knew very little about them. Strange kid that I was, I never went through my mother's underwear drawer.

Today's brassieres have one or two clasps. Back then they had eight. So I'm trying to be smooth and suave like the Fonz and my fingers are fumbling around – I had no fucking clue what I was doing.

Why the hell didn't Mrs. Richmond teach *this* in Health class?!

With Rachel's kind assistance I finally was able to unhook the bra. Wow. There they were – beautiful, naked, and mine for the fondling. I could swear I heard a celestial chorus of angels sing "Climb Every Mountain" when I got my first real good look. Being able to gaze and touch and suckle Rachel Salberg's breasts every weekend kept me satisfied all the way through the holiday season.

It's shocking how naïve and inept I was. It's kind of sweet in a way – there's something to be said for preserving innocence since it can never be reclaimed, yada yada—but I can say that *now*. Back then it was just painful. I'd kiss her goodnight, drive home, and be completely confused by the conflicting intense emotions I was experiencing. On the one hand I felt rapturous, fantastic, alive. And on the other, so goddamn frustrated I could eat the steering wheel. Who was I really – the nice respectful young gentleman that was worthy of the fair maiden's trust? Or the crass cad who wanted to fuck her until the seventh graders showed up Monday morning for homeroom?

And yet, for all the angst and conflicting emotions, I would do anything just to keep those rendezvous going every Friday and Saturday night. And by *anything* I mean international folk dancing.

Twice a month we would go to a club called Zorba the Greek's on White Oak way up in Northridge. This was one of Rachel's favorite spots. Who knew there were teenagers who liked to do Armenian line dances and Israeli folk dances? Exuberant young dervishes who kicked, and spun, and dipped, and knew all the steps to *Manavu*.

This was freaking Mars.

I can't do a box step much less a Turkish wedding stomp. Yet there I was—in the line, holding hands with sweaty Greek and Israeli guys, kicking and twirling, and hating every single nanosecond of it.

My parents knew me all too well. They asked where I was going one Saturday night and when I muttered, "International Folk Dancing" they fell on the floor laughing. Dad asked, "Do you have protection?" and I said, "No, if I break an ankle, I break an ankle."

I actually did have protection, not that I ever used it. Having a rubber deteriorating in your wallet was a badge of honor. Gary and I split a pack. That was a scene – the two of us *Lotharios* at the drug counter going through different brands and sizes and features. "Do we want Latex? This one is flavored. Why would we need one that's flavored?" I just would have felt more comfortable if Goodyear or

Firestone or some company I had ever heard of made these things.

We split a pack of twelve. Then one night when my parents were out and my brother was asleep I set about learning how to put one on. It's a good thing I had six. But I was eventually able to figure it out without having to call Gary or Mrs. Richmond. (*That* would have been a great call. "Hello, Mrs. R.? Yes, I'm taking out your daughter Becky Saturday night and wondered if you could walk me through putting on a condom?")

Eventually Mom and Dad wanted to meet this girl who could drag me to folk dance clubs. Those can be incredibly awkward scenes, but I wasn't worried. First of all, I knew they'd be thrilled that I had *any* girlfriend. And secondly, Rachel was a very substantial young lady; she certainly was no slut (despite my pleading).

So they invited her to dinner. And I must say they went all out. I had warned them that Rachel kept kosher and when we entered the house I couldn't believe it. It's as if we stepped into *Fiddler On The Roof.* There was the full Sabbath table set—candles, wine, challah, two sets of plates and silverware. Chicken from a kosher butcher. Shocked, I took Mom aside and said, "How much research did you do on this?" My parents were not just *Delicatessen Jews*; they were *Delicatessen Section of Costco Jews.*

But I was quite touched that my folks went to that effort to make a great first impression. Which they did. So did Rachel, just by being herself. Oh, if it were only that easy when I met her parents.

Rachel's father (stepfather actually) was really strange. And he was the good one. Rachel's mom was a psychopath. A yelling, screaming, scary, loose cannon of a woman. Her profession, by the way: 4th grade teacher in the L.A. School System. Rachel also had a little stepbrother, Warren – four years younger—but since he was the product of the two of them, he was clearly the favored child.

I went to their house for dinner. Her stepfather barely looked at me, or made eye contact with anybody. Warren was singing to himself. It was incredibly annoying and rude, but no one thought to scold the little precious. Mom was sweet as pie until Rachel said she was out of shampoo or some such innocuous thing, and for whatever reason it just set her mother off. She started screaming, right there at the table. I wanted to crawl into a hole. Rachel and the rest of the family just took it in stride, continuing to eat or look down at their plates. After a few minutes of insane shrieking, the storm passed and her mom settled down. There was awkward silence for a moment and then she returned to her sweet self and asked me where was I Bar Mitzvahed. Now I know why Warren sang at the table.

After dinner, we repaired to the den and watched *The Andy Williams Show* with his special guest, Janos Prohaska doing his beloved "Cookie Bear" character.

I apparently passed the test because Rachel wasn't forbidden to see me.

Not that she would have obeyed anyway. I saw a little window into Rachel that night – a steely determination, impervious to intimidation or guilt trips. She was very headstrong, as I would soon learn first-hand.

America's Rebels: The Smothers Brothers

The Smothers Brothers Comedy Hour premiered on CBS. Tommy and Dick Smothers rose from the folk music ranks but with a spin. They did comedy. Gentle and wholesome, and they still played banjos but comedy nonetheless. CBS figured they'd be the perfect hosts for a variety show geared towards Middle America.

Boy, was CBS wrong.

The Smothers Brothers Comedy Hour evolved into the hippest show on television. And later, the most controversial. With edgy young writers like Steve Martin on board, the humor was biting and satiric. Very anti-establishment. As if Lenny Bruce became a folksinger. Musical guests included Joan Baez, the Doors, Jefferson Airplane, the Who, and for the first time since he was blacklisted in the '50s – Pete Seeger. CBS was expecting Patti Page or the Lennon Sisters. Hundred-year-old Seeger caused a huge stir when he sang "Waist Deep in the Big Muddy," an anti-war folk song. CBS censored it on his first appearance but allowed it on his second.

That was just one of many battles between the Smothers Brothers (primarily Tommy, who was the creative force of the show) and network censors. Despite its high ratings, especially among teens, CBS cancelled the show two years later. It was just too much trouble. (If they were on *today* getting those numbers in the key 18-34 demographic, they could show a snuff film live and still stay on the air.)

I loved its subversive humor. So much so that I wrote the Smothers Brothers a letter offering my services as a writer. What a coup for them to get a high school kid with no experience and no idea what a script even looked like! I got back an autographed picture. I guess that meant no. I loved the show anyway.

(Fifteen years later I won my first Writers Guild Award and the presenter was... Tommy Smothers. How cool was that? Now I have two autographed pictures.)

Dear Applicant

I walked into the house one crisp November afternoon following basketball practice and was greeted by my ecstatic mother waving a letter. "You're going to UCLA!" she exclaimed. "You got in!" I looked at the letter, addressed to me (she had ripped open the envelope – the hell with steaming it open), and sure enough, I had been accepted. It was from Chancellor Young, who wrote: "Dear applicant, I'd like to *personally* welcome you to UCLA."

So that was it. Settled. I was going to UCLA. Dad came home, we gathered the family, and all went to Monty's steak house to celebrate. We had no problem getting a table. Business was very light that night as I recall. Not much time to admire all the sports memorabilia on display in the foyer. For dessert my parents splurged and ordered Baked Alaska. It was presented with great flair, blue flames shooting high into the air. Gee, I hope they had insurance.

When the letter from Cal Berkeley arrived (also *personally* welcoming this applicant) it was treated the same way those "*You may have won a million dollars!*" missives from the Publisher's Clearing House were treated. The only rejection I received was from Stanford. I seriously doubt if I would have gone there anyway and the cost was exorbitant, but screw those bastards!

Rachel's stepfather didn't want to pay for a college education (he wasn't just a milquetoast, he was also a dick) so she settled for Pierce Jr. College (Cow Tech).

(In later years Rachel would attend UCLA and get her doctorate there. Meanwhile, stepdad would die.)

As expected, most everyone stayed in California. Only one was headed east. Brainiac Lloyd Stoolman got into Princeton and was actually *going*. This seemed amazing to us. We didn't think kids from California were even allowed to visit Princeton.

Flash forward: Just before my ten-year reunion in 1978 I read a terrific book called *What Really Happened to the Class of '65* by Michael Medved and David Wallechinsky. It followed members of the graduating class of Palisades High. Like Taft, Pali High was in an upper-middle class neighborhood in Los Angeles. The tales of their students were fascinating; filled with adventure, travel, and self-discovery. I couldn't wait to hear my classmate's stories. What a disappointment. A few of the girls led interesting lives but for the guys it was all the same – they went to college, they got jobs, and now live within five miles of Taft.

The difference in those three years was of course the draft and the escalation of the Vietnam War. We didn't have the luxury of spending a "gap" year in Europe after graduation or opening a tuxedo shop and becoming the czar of rental formalwear. For us it was college or Charlie Cong. From 1965-1970 college enrollment increased 30%.

So "What Really Happened to the Class of 68?" We're all still paying off college loans.

In The Hour of Not Quite Rain

The new counterculture was not just making waves in music and society; it was making *radio* waves as well. FM had been around for over two decades, but no one ever listened. Despite its superior fidelity, FM was the ugly stepchild AM kept locked in the closet. FM stations tended to play elevator music. If a company owned both an AM and an FM, the FM would just simulcast the AM's programming, thereby picking up an additional eight listeners.

On Friday, April 7, 1967 former Top 40 disc jockey, Tom Donahue, first signed on a brand new format on KMPX-FM, San Francisco. Free-form underground radio. No jingles. No fast-talking disc jockeys. No pop hits. Long neglected album cuts from the new cutting edged bands like the Grateful Dead, the Doors, and Jefferson Airplane would finally get radio exposure. Disc jockeys were allowed to choose their own music, put sets of five or six songs together, blending various styles and genres. And unlike Top 40 disc jockeys, who were high energy and always trying to generate excitement, KMPX announcers were low key, mellow, and (okay, let's just say it) stoned. Howard Hessman, later to play Dr. Johnny Fever on *WKRP In Cincinnati*, was one of the early KMPX staffers.

We're always told that young people have short attention spans. They want their entertainment in three-minute bytes – whether it's music videos or YouTube videos. But in the '60s we craved longer album cuts. Of course many boomers were in a drug-induced haze and had no clue whether a song lasted seven minutes or seven seconds.

More 1967 polarization: singles vs. albums.

In November, Donahue and his future wife were invited to install his alternative rock format in Southern California on KPPC-FM, Pasadena, owned by a church with studios in the basement of the church (they really were "underground" radio). Their signal was practically non-existent. I couldn't even hear it out in Woodland Hills. There was a toy back then called "Mr. Microphone," which was a cheesy plastic mic attached to a tiny transmitter allowing you to broadcast maybe the length of an Impala. That would have been an improvement over KPPC's real transmitter – an antenna atop the two-story building next door. The station registered barely a blip on the ratings radar screen. Yet it was laying the groundwork for a whole new revolution in radio.

Meanwhile, KHJ was still a powerhouse on the AM dial. And I'm sure their studios were state-of-the-art—the Starship Enterprise only showier. KHJ was housed in a cool looking art deco building next door to Paramount Studios, right in the very heart of glamorous Hollywood. Would you expect anything less?

I had always wanted to see KHJ's studios but they had a strict *no visitors* policy. Record promotion men were not allowed in, much less lowly listeners. Several times I wrote the program director, Ron Jacobs, asking if I could get a tour. "No" was always the reply.

Finally, I hit upon an idea. One of KHJ's programming features was "constant contests." All of their promotions were very clever and the minute a winner was announced for one, a new one would take its place. Having to dream up all these promotions must've been a bitch.

Here's an example: The "Words" contest. Listeners were invited to send in original song lyrics and the winning entry would be put to music and appear on the next Buffalo Springfield album. Every hour the Bossjocks would read another stupefying finalist. You may think Bob Dylan is the voice of our generation. But I would submit to you it is…

Micki Callen of Reseda. Here's her winning entry (beating out 15,000 other poets), "In The Hour of Not Quite Rain."

In the hour of not quite rain

When the fog was fingertip high

The moon hung suspended

In a singular sky

Deeply and beyond seeing

Not wishing to intrude

Bathed in its own reflection

The water mirrored the moon

The tumbling birds have now sobered

From the leaves of their nursery

Like shadowy, quiet children

Watching sleepily

So there you go.

Anyway, my idea: I wrote Mr. Jacobs saying I had twenty great contest ideas and I would be willing to share them for merely a tour of the station. A week letter I received a response. I was to call Mitch Fisher, the promotions director, and he would take me up on my offer. I quickly called and a meeting was set for 4:00 the next day. I was ECSTATIC. Then it hit me – shit! I've got to come up with twenty contest ideas tonight.

Somehow I did and 24 hours later I was actually admitted into the Fortress of Solitude. As Mr. Fisher escorted me to his office I fully expected spears to shoot out from the walls. He dutifully took down my ideas and even feigned interest. Then the moment I had waited for for three years (which, for a teenager is like twenty years in grown-up time)—he asked if I wanted a tour. Does *water mirror the moon?*

He led me down more hallways. The place was a maze. A left here, a right here, another left, and finally I was led into the sacred on-air control room. The disc jockey sat across the glass from the engineer who played all the records, commercials, whatever. Through the glass – in person—was the Real Don Steele. Certainly my impression was colored by how much I revered the sound that came out of this booth, but I have to say, in all honesty, the KHJ studios were the biggest shit pile I had ever seen. Old outdated equipment. Cartridge machines that college stations no longer used. A transmitter that said, "Hail to the Kaiser!" No wonder they never let anyone see this.

It was all just a façade. A smokescreen. The Wizard of Boss.

But that's the power and magic of radio. You can create an entire world out of nothing. And that's why KPPC, hunkered down in a musty church basement with turntables powered by hamster wheels was soon to challenge the mighty KHJ.

Imagination is a level playing field.

Okay, I'll admit – I was a little disappointed after all that. But then, KHJ never used any of my contest ideas so they couldn't have been that ecstatic over me either.

I left the station at about 5:30. It was already dark.

The moon hung suspended

In a singular sky

New Year's Revelation

Daytime temperatures dropped into the frigid 60's. Christmas vacation was just around the corner. I was going to work full-time again at Wallichs but this time as an album salesman so with commissions I was going to rake it in. The week before Christmas I worked 10:00 AM – midnight seven days a week. And as I had anticipated, I made more money that one week than I ever had in my entire life. $345! I almost killed myself, but it was sure worth it!

I was also helped by the Beatles' new release, *Magical Mystery Tour*. Again, they blew everybody away. Some cuts like "Strawberry Fields Forever" were astonishing, but others like "I Am the Walrus" were starting to cross into Whackoville.

How much better are these lyrics...

Yellow matter custard

Dripping from a dead dog's eye

... from these?

The tumbling birds have now sobered

From the leaves of their nursery

I think it was time for John to tiptoe away from the medicine cabinet.

But like *Sgt. Pepper*, *Magical Mystery Tour* was a runaway number one. We couldn't order enough copies. Although, I sheepishly must admit, on more than one occasion a sweet elderly lady would ask me to recommend an album and on Christmas morning a thirteen or fourteen-year-old girl would excitedly open her present under the tree and see that Grandma had given her the Frank Zappa & Mothers of Invention *Freak Out!* album (which of course included the "Ritual Dance of the Child-Killer").

A few days before we were let out of school, I was sitting with Rachel and casually asked what she'd like to do New Year's Eve? She said she had other plans.

Say what?!

Rachel went away every summer to Camp Ramah, a Jewish summer camp not far from Santa Barbara. She had graduated to camp counselor and had made plans in September to reunite with all her other Camp Ramah counselor friends on New Year's Eve. I said, "Well, okay. I'll just come with you." She said that wouldn't be a good idea. Needless to say, I was angry and very hurt.

I reminded her that we were essentially going *together* (a bond as sacred as going *steady*), but she remained steadfast. This was that icy stubborn side I just caught a whiff of earlier. Rachel maintained that no one was to bring a guest, and she was not going to be an exception. She was very sorry, and it was nothing personal, but this was the way it had to be.

I didn't know how to respond. I cared way too much about her to want to just break up, but still I was terribly injured; it seems my feelings weren't as important as keeping this date with her Camp Ramah pals. I walked away in a daze.

I then started asking around about this Camp Ramah. What I learned disturbed me even further. For the younger kids it was a regular summer camp, but for the counselors it was a little fuck farm. Holy shit!

I confronted Rachel with this. She did not deny it but maintained that she was still a virgin. Yet when cornered she admitted that she had *fooled around* with some of these boys. What the hell did *that* mean? She wouldn't be specific. But she insisted she cared for me much more than she did for any of them. Was that supposed to be comforting? This touched off an argument, as you might have guessed.

She accused me of holding to a double standard. It was okay for me to be experienced but not her. "Back up, " I said, "What makes you think that I'm so experienced?" "Eleanor," she said. "Eleanor?" She just figured I had to be getting laid, otherwise why would anyone with even an ounce of self respect date such a whacko as Eleanor? For several months yet. This argument was not going well for me. I was forced to swallow my pride and admit that no, I did not lose my virginity—or pretty much anything else—to Eleanor. Then a thought occurred. Even though I fumbled with Rachel's bra and my eyes almost popped out of my head upon seeing her breasts, she thought I was *experienced?* "Well," she shrugged, "I just assumed you were *really* klutzy with her." At what point do I just throw myself in front of a bus?

We took the argument to the very brink of breaking up but both backed off. We would take a break from each other and see where we stood in a week or so.

But the thought of her going to that party just stuck in my craw. I knew she didn't want me tagging along because her summer boyfriend (or friends) would be there – guys who have touched her in places that I have yet to touch. And I went goddamn

International Folk dancing, for Crissakes!

So my response to this was to ask Rachel's best friend, Cheri, out for New Year's Eve and take her to Disneyland. Hell hath no fury like an immature 17 year-old. Looking back, of course it was an asinine thing to do, but some best friend of Rachel's that she'd even agree to go.

At midnight fireworks lit up the night sky over the Magic Kingdom. Nine million teenagers cheered wildly (all in jackets, ties or dresses – the Disneyland dress code not taking into account that it was 45 degrees and all the girls froze).

Spontaneously, as everyone else seemed to pair off and kiss, I kissed Cheri. It turned out to be a pretty smoldering kiss. I felt a little guilty after and admitted that during the kiss I was thinking of Rachel. She said that's okay. She was thinking of someone else too. I didn't ask who.

1967 was a turbulent but exciting year, and I had the highest hopes that 1968 was going to be even better. How fitting that I was in Fantasyland.

Make Up Petting

I woke up to watch to the Rose Parade. This was the first year we had a color TV so the whole family gathered around, oohing and ahhhing at the colors. Of course, we could also *go* to the Rose Parade. Pasadena is only thirty miles from Woodland Hills. But there was never a lot of enthusiasm for it. You have to get up in the middle of the night, fight the traffic, camp out in freezing temperatures. Much better to watch it on television; even a black-and-white. But there's the dirty little secret only the locals know. The floats are on display for three days at a local Pasadena park. You see them up close, get much better snapshots, and there are not 100,000 Indiana Hoosiers driving rental cars ahead of you, completely lost. This is where I would have taken Rachel if we weren't fighting. See? That'll teach *her*.

She and I got together that night to talk. She said she had a terrible time at the party, felt very bummed out, and asked if I did too? I told her yes. What I didn't tell her was that my depression wasn't strictly because of *her*. When Cheri and I went on the Mark Twain riverboat for our ten-minute cruise around Tom Sawyer's island, Louis Armstrong was playing on the ship. On the one hand, it was an honor to see him; on the other – Jesus, the great Louis

Armstrong had to play a gig at fucking Disneyland? That was truly sad.

Rachel and I worked things out, but with the understanding that during our make out sessions I was going to get at least as far as the Camp Ramah counselors. She thought that was fair. But of course she never admitted just how far that was. And how does one ask? "So did they get to like second base?" "Third but only with a good hard slide on a close play?"

There's nothing like make-up petting. I got to see and explore the uh, bottom half. I won't go into details, but suffice it to say it was great for me, reeeeally great for her.

So we were a happy couple again. And I did my best to drown out the little voice in my head that kept saying, "You *know* she gave the counselors hand jobs." Third base with a big lead.

The Graduate

I seem to find reasons every year to hate my birthday. This year it was having to register with the Selective Service board and maybe die in Vietnam. But on the flip side, dinner at Monty's was lovely. Those flaming desserts are spectacular! They really should have some fire extinguishers on hand – just to, y'know, be *safe*.

I went to see Eugene McCarthy speak at the Topanga Plaza. 1968 was a presidential election year and McCarthy, a Democratic senator from Minnesota, fired the first shot. He ran on an anti-Vietnam platform. At the time this was revolutionary. No one, including him, seriously thought he could wrestle the Democratic nomination away from sitting President Lyndon Johnson, but he hoped to exert a little pressure on the administration to stop the war. He was persuasive and charismatic, and it was just so refreshing to hear a politician whose views seemed so forward thinking. Especially coming on the heels of Republican hardliner, Ronald Reagan, seizing Sacramento. Like I said, no one thought Eugene McCarthy had a chance, but for once a voice protesting the war belonged to an elected official not some bearded college student with a placard or a wasted waif inserting a flower in a rifle barrel.

You'd think this was a sign that the country was becoming more socially and politically conscious, less frivolous. But then…

Laugh In premiered in January.

This show became a national sensation. Looking back, it was maybe the unfunniest sketch comedy show ever. Basically the format was a series of musty vaudeville and burlesque jokes and blackouts punctuated by groovy go-go dancers and (awful) stand-up routines by the comedy team of Dan Rowan & Dick Martin. Yet, at the time, American viewers (me included) found this stuff fall-on-the-floor funny.

There were a few bright spots – the young perky Goldie Hawn was a regular, as was Gary Owens (the baritone old-time announcer), Henry Gibson, and the wondrous Lily Tomlin (who wisely bolted early). But the downsides – ugh! One of the show's signature sets was a wall in mod design with all these closed windows. Cast members would pop open a window, deliver a leaden punch line, and shut the window. What was I laughing at… week after week?

"*Hilarious*" catch phrases that caught on from the show: "Sock it to me," "Look that up in your Funk & Wagnells," "Very eeenteresting," "Here come da Judge," and "You bet your bippy."

For the next two years this was the runaway number one show in the country – every Monday night on NBC. And again, I was laughing right along with everyone else. I just can't fathom why. (I do have a great *Laugh In* story but you'll have to wait until 1969.)

Another significant aspect of *Laugh In* was that it took the counterculture, sanitized it, and turned it into mainstream-culture. Not that they were alone in that regard. When the Beatles went to India to find enlightenment from the heralded Maharishi Yogi and only came away wearing Nehru jackets, Nehru jackets became the rage. These were low-length tailored coats with stand-up Mandarin collars, usually buttoned in the front. The very second they were no longer in vogue they were considered ridiculous and no one who owned one dared wear it in public. Except Sammy Davis Jr. who owned 200 of them, so by God he was going to get his money's worth. They were also very popular among Bond super-villains. Dr. No, Ernst Blowfeld, Kamal Khan, and Hugo Drax all sported them. No wonder audiences cheered when they were killed.

On a rainy January Saturday night Rachel and I saw *The Graduate* at the Village Theater in Westwood, a rather timely movie since, as a winter class, we would be graduates ourselves in just a couple of weeks. If ever a movie spoke to our generation it was this one. We faced an uncertain future in a society whose values we questioned. Dustin Hoffman, as the aimless college graduate, captured perfectly the angst and confusion we all felt. But that wasn't the good stuff. Not for me. What had such a huge impact on this young lad was that he slept with his parents' friend, Mrs. Robinson. Ohmygod! There's hope for me and Mrs. Nussbaum! I sat through that seduction in stunned amazement as my every fantasy played out on the screen. How did they know? One of my issues was always that I considered myself a little weird, had thoughts and desires not shared by the rest of my peers. And to see that hey, I'm not the only teenager who wants to fuck a married woman who plays Pan with my mother was a huge relief.

Coo coo cha choo, Mrs. Robinson, you are the patron saint of MILFs.

A film professor I know says that today's students are completely bored by *The Graduate*. The pace is way too slow and the subject matter resonates not at all. So it's hard to convey just how significant the movie was to all of us. But trust me, everyone at Taft saw it… four or five times.

With our graduation only weeks away, the big question was what were we seniors going to do to celebrate Grad Night? This is only a problem for us screwy winter classes. June graduates all go to

Disneyland. But what's there to do in January? Rachel was on the Grad Night committee and actually had a brilliant idea. Why not do something at Universal Studios? At the time they offered their tram tour but nothing else. Rachel thought Universal could be like Disneyland – a theme park with the theme being movies. For our one overnight she suggested opening up the old Western street or New York street. Universal turned her down flat. They thought it was a preposterous idea. Short sighted on their part? You bet your bippy.

The Grad Night plan we settled on was one my administration would have heartily endorsed, had I been elected – we did nothing.

As it turned out, Universal would not have been an ideal spot because it poured the night of our graduation. The ceremony was held in the stuffy gym, family members sat uncomfortably on the backless wooden bleachers, and I didn't have to give a speech. I can't claim to feel real nostalgic that night. For some graduates this marked the end of the happiest period of their lives, and my sense is that some of them knew it. So yeah, there were a few homecoming queen and starting quarterback tears. How incredibly sad that there are people whose lives peak at seventeen. Imagine spending the next six or seven decades disappointed and disillusioned. And these were the classmates we envied.

Personally, I was ready to get out. Where once Taft felt so vast and adult; now it seemed confining and stunting. I do have some lovely memories, but never did I have any desire to go back and "relive the good old days." In fact, after I drove off the campus that night, it wasn't until thirty years later that I finally returned. Through the years I've managed to keep up with a number of college friends, but there are only a handful of high school classmates I've bothered to stay in touch with.

Grad Night consisted of watching the sun come up from the

Hughes Jr. High parking lot. And getting to third base. *That's* the graduation I cherish.

PART FOUR

At Least Clyde Got Laid

No longer being in high school meant I could finally grow my hair long. Since I was still rail thin, within a few weeks I looked like a feather duster. Nana Lil was of course, horrified. "We've lost him!" was, I believe, her mantra. My parents weren't too thrilled either but recognized at least that this was the style of the day. The most common attack from people was always, "You look like a girl!" The reply I always wanted to give was, "Yes, but a *cute* girl?" It seemed like Paul McCartney, Davey Jones of the Monkees, and every other guy who looked like a cute girl got more action from *real* cute girls than guys who looked like guys.

Rachel liked the new do. And I think it brought us closer together. We began sharing the same Aqua Net hair spray.

UCLA was on a quarter system so I wasn't slated to begin college until the end of March. That meant I had six weeks off to do nothing. And that's exactly what I did. Rachel began Pierce Jr. College in February. I would meet her after class. Otherwise, I got in a car accident and went to movies.

I somehow hit a pole and crunched the right corner of the Comet... ironically in the same parking lot I learned how to drive (obviously not too well). We figured the damage to be about $800. If I reported it to insurance I'd still have to fork over the $500 deductible and my *already-high-cause-I'm-a-teenager* rates would skyrocket. Fortunately, I had saved my Wallichs money. I checked the classifieds (the *Flintstones'* answer to Craig's List) and saw a used 1966 Mustang was available for $1300. That price seemed suspiciously reasonable, but I checked it out. She was a beauty. Cream yellow, great design, low mileage. Only one hitch – it had a nice big crease in the side.

I drove the Comet to Neider's Auto Body on Ventura Blvd. and made them a offer: fix the Mustang and I would give them the Comet. They could repair it and use it as a loaner. They went for the deal. I then talked the Mustang owner into lowering his price to $900. My savings were completely cleaned out, but now I had a car that was still in production. To this day that was my favorite car. I drove it for nine years, put 100,000 miles on it, and still have the ignition key on my key ring.

Back in the '60s hit movies would stay in theaters forever. (Of course they also weren't on Netflix On-Demand two weeks after release.) *Bonnie & Clyde* was a landmark film. At the time I didn't know that. All I knew was this was one hairy gorefest! Warren Beatty and Faye Dunaway got shot three thousand times and were a bloody mess by the time they finally hit the ground (I'm assuming dead). Not your typical Hollywood ending. But it began a trend of more realistic, more adventuresome, more original movies. The '70s would prove to be a golden age of film, but it all began in the late '60s. Today, if a movie like *Bonnie & Clyde* were a runaway hit Hollywood studios would say, "How can we bring them back for the sequel?"

Then there was *Cool Hand Luke* (one of Paul Newman's best), *Wait Until Dark* (scary as hell without a single special effect or chainsaw), *Camelot* and *In Cold Blood* (two similar book adaptations), and my favorite guilty pleasure of the year...

Valley Of The Dolls. Based on the trashy novel of the same name. I saw it at the Corbin Theater and remember lusting after Barbara Parkins (yet another Mrs. Robinson/Nussbaum fantasy), never dreaming that she'd someday become my neighbor. Everything about the movie was sleazy and appalling, so to no one's surprise, it was a smash. And then they outdid themselves in poor taste by re-releasing it in 1969 after one of its stars, Sharon Tate, was killed in the Manson murders. (More on that later. You have Goldie Hawn and Charlie Manson to look forward to.)

Winter '68 was particularly cold, gray, and wet. So when the sun broke through and the temperature shot up to 85 one Friday in early March I made a beeline to the beach. These were the days before sunscreen. By the time I drove home in the late afternoon I was burnt to a crisp. This happened to be the first night of Passover, which is traditionally celebrated by a prayer service and feast called a Seder. Levine services were breezy twenty-minute affairs. We just sort of skimmed over the program. At one point the leader is required to tell the story of Passover – essentially the movie *The Ten Commandments*. My father would tell the story of whatever sword and sandal movie he had seen last. So one year it could be *The Ten Commandments* and the next year it could be *El Cid*. The service usually lasted fifteen minutes and a good time was had by all.

This year I was invited to Rachel's family Seder. Even the loosest of clothes against my tender flesh was agony. But being the dutiful boyfriend (and having reached third base) I reported as scheduled. Rachel hugged me and I almost passed out.

The Salberg service was not like ours. Theirs took several HOURS. All in Hebrew. Midway through, I'm shivering and convulsing, which didn't seem to disturb Rachel's parents. In fact, I think I caught them smiling. Plus, Warren's singing was far more distracting. Hum an actual *song* once in a while! We finally polished off a delicious dessert of gummy macaroons, and just as I was about to excuse myself to go to the E.R., Psycho-Mom suggested we all repair to the living room for a special treat. Shit! Unless the treat was skin grafting I wanted no part of it. For the next hour, in excruciating pain, I endured slides of their summer '67 trip to exotic San Jose – a trip that didn't even include Rachel since she was at Camp Ramah fellating fellow counselors. All Jews pray that night that the Angel of Death will *"Pass over"* them. I was praying that he take me.

I was hoping my supreme sacrifice would be *rewarded* the next night, but it was not. There was clearly handwriting on the wall regarding this relationship. Either I chose to ignore it (or it was written in Hebrew and I couldn't decipher it), but the point is, there was trouble in paradise.

The Stamp Club Or the Black Panthers?

There were no weeklong orientation events and activities at UCLA when you entered in Spring Quarter. You got a map and a decal. But I did get invited to pledge a fraternity. Sigma Alpha Mu (known to some as the *Sammies*, known to all as the *Jews*) requested my presence for a barbeque at their frat house. I walked in and was immediately repulsed. I don't know what I was expecting but not a crackhouse after a raid. This place was a pigsty. A semi-conscious collection of sloths were either passed out on old threadbare couches or playing tackle football in the living room. Empty beer cans and former lamps were strewn everywhere. The place smelled like vomit. And I assume this is after they cleaned it to impress us. I was out of there in ten minutes, not that anyone noticed or cared.

Fraternities and sororities had seen better days – at least at UCLA. Maybe not at USC, which was more preppy and enrolled more Muffys and Tippys and Biffs, but in Westwood and a growing number of other campuses, where materialism and capitalism were now considered *bourgeois*, the Greek system felt passé and almost anachronistic. So not joining was no big loss. I figured among 30,000 undergraduate students and groups that ranged from the

Stamp Club to the Black Panthers I'd find *some* niche for myself.

There was the school newspaper. But no one really read it. Underground newspapers were by then the rage of rags. Published in basements with skeleton staffs of young social reformers, activists, and potheads, these papers focused on topics relevant to us – the war, radical politics, music, drugs. And there were ads for strip joints and escort services. By 1969 there were four hundred underground papers. Ours was the *L.A. Free Press.* Paperboys would stand on street corners chanting, *"Don't be a creep, buy a Freep!"* What attracted me most were the political cartoons. Drawings by wildly imaginative cartoonists like Ron Cobb and Gilbert Shelton appeared frequently. I made a mental note to seek out the *Free Press* once I was settled in college, but I never did.

I was very excited to get started already. How many times can you see *Valley Of The Dolls*? (Three.) UCLA seemed so very *grown up* to me. Large lecture halls, no one taking attendance, no hall passes. You were treated like an adult. I'd visit Rachel at Pierce and it was high school with cows. I felt proud to be accepted by an educational institution that expected you to perform without having to monitor you. The downside of course, is that it was so big no one really gave a shit whether you passed or not.

I was to be a commuter so I petitioned for a parking permit. There are several large parking structures conveniently located on the campus. I was assigned to Lot 32, which was on the far end of Westwood Village, about a mile and a half away. I wanted big and impersonal? That's what I got. Shuttle buses would transport you to and from, but you still had to add an hour onto your daily commute.

Getting your classes at Taft was hard enough when you had to run around the gym like rats in a Skinner box. At UCLA you literally *ran* for your classes. At 8:00 AM on the appointed day, registration was open and you went to the classroom itself, exchanged cards if there was an opening, and moved on to the next class. Did I mention you could fit Liechtenstein in UCLA's food court?

Naturally you line up first for the class you need the most or is the hardest to get and go from there. Or, if you're not a clueless freshman like me, you get three friends to stake out the other classes for you. I did it all on my own. And I got all my classes, thank you. Introductory Psychology, Natural Science, Logic, and American Lit. Only problem was my classes were Monday/Wednesday/Friday at 8:00 AM and 2:00 PM, and Tuesday/Thursday at 9:00 AM and 3:30 PM. Not exactly a compact schedule. Another trick I would learn is not to take classes by subject but by time. By my senior year I was only taking classes that were offered between noon and three even if they were Metaphysics 2 or Beginning Urdu.

I never liked school. So I knew that once I got my undergraduate degree I was done. That took a certain amount of pressure off. There was no need to get all A's and B's so I could get into grad school. I just needed passing grades and that's pretty much what I got. Looking back, I wish I had taken better advantage of my college experience. What I came away with after four years was a better understanding of how to play the system, not how to broaden my knowledge.

I didn't know for sure what I wanted to be when/if I grew up, but I knew this much – it had to be an *elective*. When you go to high school, you are forced to take strenuously boring classes like Math and English and usually one fun elective – like drawing or drama. But when you get out into the real world no one is forcing you take those dry required subjects anymore. Your vocation can be an *elective*. So for me it was something in the arts – radio, TV, film, Broadway, sportscasting, cartooning, comedy. And with that in mind, what did I major in at UCLA?

Psychology.

I wanted to enroll as a TV or film major but my father wisely said those were trades I could learn on the job. If I was going to a major university I should make the most of it and really get an academic education. It meant a more rigorous curriculum, but I could see his point. Plus, he was paying for the whole ride.

As a resident of California, here's what that meant: $83 tuition a quarter. Counting books and other miscellaneous items, I think my parents sent me through four years at the University of California at Los Angeles for less than $2000 total. Today I imagine the application costs more than that.

But I must say I was able to put my B.A. in Psychology to good use. I wrote Frasier and Lilith's psychobabble so much easier as a result.

The Mighty KLA

For the first few weeks my routine was the same. Leave for UCLA at 6:30 in the morning; get home around 5:00. I killed the many hours between classes in the Powell Library doing homework or eating at the student union. I talked to no one. I knew no one.

None of the campus groups seemed an ideal fit. The big one was SDS (Students for a Democratic Society), but they were a little too militant and angry for me. I wanted a group that grumbled but then went out for pizza.

And then an organization I wanted no part in was the ROTC (Reserve Officers Training Corps). This was a military officers training program for college students. They would march around, polish rifles, and other fun army-related activities. But in light of the pervasive anti-Vietnam sentiment among students, everyone wanted the ROTC removed from campus. There were protests. Since being a military officer was on my *things-to-do* list right behind ski jumping and becoming the Pope, I steered clear of the ROTC. Years later I learned I really missed out. Tennis star, Arthur Ashe was a member at the time. Just think, I could have spit-shined latrines with Arthur Ashe!

None of these groups, clubs, or fighting machines matched my sensibilities. Until...

I stumbled into the campus radio station, KLA.

Finally! Thin, fat, short, gawky, self-conscious, tall, neurotic, uncoordinated, socially inept, bespectacled outcasts – *these* were my peeps!!

No one at high school shared my interest in radio. I had, however, developed a small network of pen pals from around the country who were also on the same AM/FM wavelength. I would send letters to radio stations around the country asking for samples of their programming – tapes of broadcasts or jingles. A few complied. It was here that I was first introduced to the wonders of Dan Ingram on WABC, New York. This was the funniest disc jockey I had ever heard. And lightening-quick. I was in awe, had never heard anything like him. Robert W. Morgan on KHJ (a first-class wit himself) would say five or ten funny things every hour. Dan Ingram would say ten or twenty funny things every five *minutes*. Totally irreverent and fearless, he would poke fun at the station, the music, himself, even the commercials. And his humor was wildly off-center, almost borderline sick. The first tape I ever heard of him, he signed on by talking about a back X-Ray he had just had. He read the results over the air then said, "I just keep thinking about Roy Campanella and how we've all been very cruel to him." What??? Where the hell did *that* come from??? As much as I loved growing up in Southern California, I do envy those kids in New York who were treated to this inspired lunacy four hours every day.

Most of the stations ignored my letters, a few sent tapes, and a few referred me to other radio enthusiasts who had sent them similar requests. I became pen pals with four of these fellow nerds. One in Long Island, one in New Jersey, a third in Pittsburgh, and the fourth in Florida. I would pepper them with endless questions about east coast radio; they would ask me what it's like to have a girlfriend. I'm still good friends with two of them. The others were and are too weird even for me.

So why did I wait a couple of weeks to knock on KLA's door? Because their signal was so bad I didn't even know there *was* a radio station. Broadcasting at 830 on the AM dial, its mighty signal reached a grand total of maybe fifteen dorm floors.

But you'd never know it from the on-air presentation.

KLA's programming was as ambitious as any commercial station in Los Angeles. They were on the air 24/7 with commercials, jingles, contests, a music director, and full news and sports departments. Most shifts, including midnight to six Monday through Friday were handled live. There was a very tight format and it was all student-run.

The only thing KLA did not cover was sports. Local station KMPC controlled the broadcast rights to UCLA sporting events and wanted to preserve their exclusivity. They were a 50,000-watt behemoth. They had major radio personalities like Gary Owens (one of the stars of *Laugh In*), traffic helicopters and planes, a multi-million dollar state-of-the-art facility, and in addition to the Bruins they carried the Rams and Angels. Yeah, like our little carrier-current teapot was going to make a big dent in their ratings. So I hated KMPC. They were the giant corporate enemy.

KLA broadcast from a cubbyhole against the back wall of the cavernous grand ballroom in the student union. The station had an on-air studio, production studio, newsroom, music library, office, and lobby and was approximately the size of a New Jersey Turnpike Tollbooth. But it was home.

There were no openings for disc jockeys, or anything for that matter, but I didn't care. I was happy just to hang around.

The big water cooler topic around the station was that KFWB, former king of the hill before KHJ came along, threw in the Top 40 towel and on March 11ᵗʰ (the day before the first presidential primary) flipped to an all-news format. Even though I had stopped listening this was still a blow – one of those stinging reminders that your childhood was over; even as you were still living it.

That first primary in New Hampshire proved to be a shocker. Democratic challenger Eugene McCarthy came within seven percentage points of defeating President Johnson. Nineteen days later, Johnson (who won in 1964 by a landslide) stunned the nation by announcing: *"I shall not seek, and will not accept, the nomination of my party for another term as your president."* The Vietnam "Police Action" had claimed yet another casualty. Opposition to the war was growing and getting louder while on the other side, proponents dug in their heels. Johnson's withdrawal from the race set the stage for one of the most turbulent and tragic periods in American history.

I was at KLA the night Johnson made his bombshell announcement, getting ready to go out to Gomi's coffee shop with several other staff members where we would discuss the merits of KHJ's new "Double Golden" jingle for six hours. We cheered. You could hear cheering from every corner of the campus.

The euphoria lasted all of five days.

The Unthinkable

On April 4th Dr. Martin Luther King Jr. was gunned down at a motel in Memphis, Tennessee. He died an hour later. I can't describe the shock. How could the unthinkable happen… twice? First Kennedy and then King. What kind of country is this that assassinates its most compassionate leaders? There was no way to make sense of what had happened. Of course, there never is.

I called Rachel's house. This was definitely a night to be with the one you thought you love. Momzilla answered. Rachel was not home. Modern Dance class practice. So much for that. Babette was there to console me, though. I watched the coverage with my family, Babette's furry head in my lap. For all the talk about the so-called "generation gap," our parents were having just as much difficulty processing all this as we were.

Rachel and I finally met up the next day for lunch at Pierce. Dance practice apparently hadn't gone well. No one was in the mood. They probably should just have called it off. Wiseass me retorted, "Yeah, well, now you guys know for the next assassination." Little did I know that in less than three months there would *be* one. Rachel actually smiled. I think she was happy for any kind of levity. We held hands and shared our feelings and by the end we were both blinking back tears. You didn't have to march in rallies or distribute handouts to feel a real connection to this man and his movement.

King represented hope in the world. Change and improvement and progress, at a time of uncertainty, violence, and growing anger. His kind is very rare, as evidenced by the fact that we haven't seen one like him since.

Riots erupted in a hundred cities. The feeling of intense sadness and disbelief hung like a cloud over the entire nation. For days, maybe weeks, at UCLA you got the sense that everyone was just going through the motions. The entire tone of the university changed. Attending classes felt more like punching-in for work. Not that UCLA was primarily a party school anyway, but the campus vibe became decidedly more subdued. I imagine the Sammies only went through one keg a night instead of four.

Usually news events happened on a parallel plane. We'd hear about the Tet Offensive in Vietnam or a Delta airliner hi-jacked to Cuba, talk about it a little, and then pretty much continue on with our own lives. Some of these events would have implications, but they would seep slowly into our daily existences. For the most part it was business, classes, international folk dancing as usual. King's death was one of the few events that had an immediate and lasting impact on our day-to-day lives.

The Beach Boys set down the hallucinogens for the moment and tried to recapture the California Myth with their new song, "Do It Again" but that wave had crested.

I must say though, part of me did miss those more innocent times, when we surfed (well, when *they* surfed) and the beach was the place to go, not a protest rally at the Federal building.

Another big hit was "Age of Aquarius" by the Fifth Dimension from the groundbreaking new Broadway musical, *Hair* (groundbreaking in that there were rock songs and brief nudity. This was quite a departure from *Hello Dolly*.) We were told we were entering a new astrological cycle, filled with wonder and love. That's "groovy" except we already *were* in the Age of Aquarius. It lasts 2,150 years.

My Radio Debut That No One Heard – Thank God

On Sunday, April 28th we went on Daylight Savings Time. Clocks were moved ahead one hour. That meant that whoever was doing the 6:00-noon shift on KLA that day was really starting at 5:00 AM. Big surprise, no one wanted to work that shift. So I volunteered. Anything to get on the air, even if it was at an ungodly hour on a station that at best could be heard by ten people.

Vin DiBona, the student program director, was all too happy to let me do it. Truth is, he would have said yes to someone with Tourette's if that were his only option. (DiBona, by the way, drifted into television production, formed his own company, and created a little show called *America's Funniest Home Videos*. The most successful people in radio are the ones who got out of it.)

I was elated! For days I went into the production studio and practiced – talking right up to the vocals of songs, rehearsing ad libs, doing dry run weather forecasts. Come Sunday morning I was READY. The next Dan Ingram had ARRIVED.

And I was awful.

It didn't help having a witty line over "Macarthur Park" when I hit the wrong button and played "Aquarius" instead… at the wrong speed. Eventually I got the hang of it, and by the end of six hours I was competent enough that Vin offered me a regular time slot – Saturday and Sunday night from midnight to six. (No one wanted to do that one either.) The good news was Vin let me prerecord the shows. So between juggling four classes, commuting, Armenian dancing, and a part-time job, I also worked in twelve hours weekly of disc jockeying. Thank God none of those tapes still exist. My attempts at being endlessly hilarious fell a little short. Dan Ingram I was not. Laura Ingraham I was not. But doing those shows was the most fun I had that quarter, which tells you I still hadn't consummated with Rachel. I soon would, but at a cost.

And Finally...Robert F. Kennedy

June was the worst. First I got the news that Gary was moving to Dallas. He had been pretty scarce since graduation, working full-time for his father who printed church annuals. I guess there were more God fearing people in Dallas who desired that kind of keepsake. (*"Oooh, do you think I could get Jesus to sign my yearbook?"*) I had made other friends recently from KLA, but it's a blow to lose your best friend.

At least I had my adoring girlfriend.

Uh...well...er...um...

I thought Rachel wasn't going back to Camp Ramah. She knew how uncomfortable I was with her in that den of Jewish depravity. But she got an offer she couldn't refuse. They wanted her to head their dance program... in the Pocono's—the crown jewel of the Ramah breeding farms. This was a huge honor (I was told). So Rachel would be gone for nine weeks. I was devastated. She too was very upset, but not enough to decline the offer.

For a week I walked around in a daze. And the timing couldn't be worse since it was Finals Week. Not that I was headed for the

Dean's List anyway, but I was lucky to escape that quarter with grades only slightly higher than the football team's.

Whether it was uncontrollable desire or (more likely) guilt over leaving me, Rachel and I finally did the deed. I think. It was over so quickly. Certainly too quick for the year-long build-up. But that was my fault. Still, a milestone had been reached. I figured it could only get better (I actually considered ordering "Mr. Satisfy" pills from Wolfman Jack), but the net result was my love for Rachel increased at an unrealistic insane rate. And that, of course, only made the impending separation worse.

Her flight to Philadelphia left early in the morning. I drove her to the airport. We vowed to write each other every day. She promised she'd be true. I promised to believe her. We sat in the gate waiting area (remember, there was a time when you *could*), holding hands in silence. What was there to say? At 18 a teenager thinks if he loses his girlfriend he'll never find another one. I mean, it was just dumb luck that I had found *this* one.

Boarding time arrived. There was a huge lump in my throat. We hugged. I was somewhat comforted that she was holding back tears, too. The first one to whisper, "I love you" was me. The first one to break the embrace was her. She crossed to the gate, looked back at me over her shoulder, I tried to smile and reassure her I was alright, she smiled back ruefully and then disappeared up the jet walk.

I stayed until the plane left the gate and taxied out of sight. I knew things would never be the same. And this was like the third "*things would never be the same*" revelation I'd had since December. That couldn't be good.

June 4th was the California Primary. I was part of KLA's coverage. We broke format with newscasts every half hour. Hope it didn't hurt our ratings. The mood was joyous. We were all thrilled that Bobby Kennedy had won. He was now our guy – clearly the one candidate who shared our ideals, opposition to the war, and hopes for the future (with part of that future meaning a return to the past and Camelot). We were all just waiting to carry his victory speech before heading off to Gomi's coffee shop to celebrate. Kennedy was at the Ambassador Hotel in the mid-Wilshire district, a sprawling landmark hotel.

We aired Kennedy's speech, were preparing to close up shop and suddenly the Teletype machine went bonkers. Bells rang urgently. And repeatedly. We all raced to the newsroom. This had to be some major bulletin.

It was.

Moments after Kennedy's speech, as he was leaving the Embassy Room ballroom through the pantry area of the main kitchen, he was shot along with five other people. Palestinian immigrant Sirhan Sirhan was arrested at the scene.

Senator Kennedy died the next day. As did our hopes, dreams, optimism, and faith; never to be restored really.

The other shooting victims survived. Sirhan Sirhan was convicted of murder. Most believe he acted alone although theories exist that the CIA was involved and possibly even a second shooter. Conspiracy theories replaced sex as America's favorite conversation piece.

We stayed on the air throughout the night. Our reports basically just parroted what we saw on television. And there had to be no one listening to us, but pretending to be journalists allowed us to at least cope with the initial shock. By this point we were beyond disbelief – disbelief was King's murder – this was just mind numbing. Worse than disbelief was *belief* and by the third major assassination, we were now almost anesthetized.

I got to my car at about 5:00 AM. It was still dark. I sat in empty Parking Lot 32 and just broke down crying. I cried over Kennedy (both Kennedys), Rachel, Dr. King, Gary, and probably some residual over Ann, Bev, and my aunt Charlotte who died at 39 on my twelfth birthday. Finally, as the sun came up, I drove home knowing the drill by now – two days of unrelenting media coverage you just couldn't turn off. And sadness.

The Summer Of My Discontent

Rachel and I did write to each other every day. At least at first. Her letters always had sealing wax and the letters "SWAK" (sealed with a kiss). Mine featured cartoon doodles. She was doing fine. Her bunkmates seemed nice. It rained a lot. The dance program was going very well. The food was mediocre, but on Wednesdays they had good fried chicken. I had tonsillitis. Eventually the frequency of our correspondence waned. I mean, it's understandable. How many times can you say I miss you and I need new tires? By mid-summer we had settled into a comfortable three or four letters a week. And we talked by phone twice. On Sundays they were allowed to use the pay phone at the office. But of course she couldn't talk long. There was a line of people behind her.

Still, just hearing her voice lifted my spirits. Of course I kept listening for tell-tale signs. Was she a little guarded? A little reserved? Was I a paranoid nut case? All signs indicated she was the same ol' Rachel. But the truth is nothing could assuage my suspicions. After all, she was spending the summer at Caligula's country estate. I'm sure these suspicions were based more on my feelings of inadequacy than any real distrust of Rachel. It never once occurred to me that

Rachel might be worried that *I* was seeing other people. She had no reason to, of course—I never dated once that entire summer (not even with her best friend)—but the thought never crossed my mind that she might be curious. She had me so wrapped around her little finger.

Here's what we were buying that summer (based on the commercials heard one afternoon on KHJ): Coors beer ("It's the water"), Hamm's beer ("From the land of sky blue water"), Schlitz beer ("When you're out of Schlitz, you're out of beer"), Apple beer (non alcoholic – probably as God awful as it sounds), Wind Song perfume ("Wind Song stays on your mind" – Eleanor's brand of choice. You're supposed to dab a drop behind your ear. She marinated in it.), Heaven Scent perfume, Sea & Ski tanning lotion, Tanya tanning lotion, Johnson & Johnson baby oil (used as tanning lotion), Rally car wax, Turtle wax, Suzuki motorcycles, Irwindale Raceway ("Funny cars!!!"), Chevron gasoline (where you get free "Hula Dollars"), Phillips gasoline (where you get free baseball books), and for the kids in the audience – Country Club Malt Liquor.

The summer of '68 is when I became a concert promoter. Most of my free time was spent at KLA. New program director, Tom Greenleigh and a few of us dedicated staff members (read: no social life) would assemble at the station. We were off the air for the summer (not that anyone would notice), but we did need to plan for the big fall launch. We sold advertising, devised contests, purchased jingles, created a slogan (*KLA/83: "The Total Sound"* – I have no idea what that means), yet still needed a real attention grabber. Tom came up with the idea of staging a concert. All the big radio stations sponsored major concerts. KRLA presented the Beatles. KHJ presented everyone else. All we needed was a major rock group, a venue, a date, a marketing plan, permits, and the capital to fund this. The bulk of the summer was spent putting this ambitious project together.

The Grassroots were a hot L.A. garage band riding the crest of several top ten hits. They had just released what would be their biggest smash, "Midnight Confessions." We were able to get them, along with several other bands, handled by the same manager. The Associated Students of UCLA finally okayed the expenditure once we assured them that all profits would go to UCLA charities. The only real hang up was Sheila James. Once an actress (she played Zelda Gilroy on *Dobie Gillis*) she was now part of ASUCLA management and had major concerns about security. (And she always wondered why Dobie was never interested in her. It's because she pulled shit like *that*!)

A venue was chosen – the roof of Parking Structure 8. Instead of renting a million chairs we just made it a "dance." I did all the artwork for the posters and ads and handled a lot of the publicity. Amazingly, the whole event was starting to come together.

Another of my assignments was to ensure that "Midnight Confessions" was a hit. So I pushed it on everybody who walked into Wallichs and called radio station listener lines a thousand times a day to request it. One time I got through to the disc jockey on KRLA who responded to my request by snarling, "Hey fuckhead, I'm playing it right now. Listen to the goddamn station once in a while, asshole!" Oops.

The summer passed slowly but there were enough diversions between concert promoting, working at Wallich's, and corresponding with my radio geek pals (none of whom signed their envelopes S.W.A.K.) to keep self-pitying to a minimum.

After only two years the Monkees television show was cancelled. Success had gone to their heads. They started to believe they were both a great rock band and gifted comedians. Turns out they were neither. By the time they realized that, the genie was out of the bottle…literally. NBC replaced them with *I Dream Of Jeanie*.

The monkeys that audiences *were* watching that summer were the ones in Stanley Kubrick's *2001: A Space Odyssey* whacking each other with bones and discovering a giant black monolith. I was one of those theatergoers, sitting in the giant Cinerama Dome in Hollywood, watching this dazzling ambitious monumental achievement in cinema and thinking, "What the hell is *this* shit?" I was expecting more of a *Star Trek* space adventure movie with fazer guns and alien villains with foreheads so big you could play racquetball on them, and instead was treated to nine hours of confusing symbolism, monoliths flying around, multi-colored lights shows, a bedroom containing Louis XIV-style décor, and finally our hero transformed into a fetus floating over the earth. Huh??? I was sooooo confused. Worse, I was soooooo bored. I know critics hail it as one of the greatest movies of all-time but I thought it was thunderously dull. Still do.

Part of my problem, I admit, was that I didn't see it stoned. Getting high was almost a prerequisite to seeing this movie, especially during the sequence where the astronaut travels in a pod through a tunnel of psychedelic lights. (To this day, if a revival theater shows *2001* they should hand out joints the way 3D movies distribute glasses.) I can't tell you how many friends absolutely raved about the film and when I asked questions about what it meant or what that monolith was for, none of them had the slightest idea. Nor did it bother any of them. Kubrick spent two years filming and editing this movie. He could have saved a lot of money and production time if he had just stuck a camera in a paint mixer.

Rachel was due to return on August 28th. I was anxiously counting the days. I'd like to say I could think of nothing else but the reality is my attention was sharply divided the week of her arrival. The Democratic National Convention was taking place in Chicago. I was always fascinated by national political conventions but this one figured to be a letdown. After all of our high hopes for Eugene McCarthy and Robert Kennedy, the presidential nomination was going to Hubert Humphrey, a decent fellow and a far better alternative than the Republican candidate, Richard Nixon, (as would have been Flipper), but HH was still a mainstream status quo politician.

Student protests, stoked by the fires of assassinations, war, civil unrest, and probably ten other things, s grew in number and intensity. Several organizations like the SDS (Students for a Democratic Society) and the Yippies moved to the forefront led by persuasive speakers like Tom Hayden (who would eventually marry Jane "Diving Board" Fonda), and political pranksters Abbie Hoffman, and Jerry Rubin. For maximum exposure they all decided to converge on Chicago to protest at the convention. They knew a photo op when they saw one.

Mayor Richard J. Daley was hardly the gracious host. He refused permits and mobilized his police force with instructions to bust heads. The protesters were confined to Grant Park.

On August 28th, the cops began beating a young protester who lowered a flag. That set off a riot. The National Guard was summoned. At one point there were 10,000 protesters and 13,000 police and guardsmen. Things got very ugly very fast. Thousands were tear-gassed and roughed up. One was killed. Protesters scrambled out of the park searching for safety. This just widened the riot area. Meanwhile, the convention was in session. The networks began shifting coverage to the riots. A shocked nation watched defenseless college kids clubbed, beaten, dragged, gassed, and thrown into paddy wagons.

On the convention podium, Connecticut senator Abe Ribicoff, in his nominating speech for George McGovern said, "With George McGovern we wouldn't have Gestapo tactics on the streets of

Chicago." Mayor Daley on the floor is reputed to have called out, "Fuck you, you Jew son of a bitch! You lousy motherfucker! Go home!"

Meanwhile, I'm watching all of this at home and becoming so furious my head is about to explode. I'm literally screaming at the television. And then in the midst of all this, I have to leave. I have to go to the airport.

I had counted the days; the hours even, until I could finally reunite with my darling Rachel. And now, as she walked off the plane and we embraced, all I could think of was "those motherfucking thugs!" On the drive home all I could talk about was the riot. Rachel was completely confused. Being in the protective bubble of summer camp, she knew very little of these incendiary events. And what happened to that sweet lovesick callow lad she said goodbye to just nine weeks before?

Both Sides Now

The upshot to the convention – Humphrey won the nomination. The chief organizers of the protest were arrested and tried as the "Chicago Seven." The judge, Julius Hoffman (no relation to Abbie) was erratic and downright crazy. The trial was a complete circus and eventually all convictions were overturned.

And the only viable candidate left for us was Pat Paulsen. Paulsen was a deadpan comic on *the Smothers Brothers Comedy Hour*. As a spoof on politics he ran for President. Paulsen was a master of double-talk (thus making him imminently qualified to be the supreme leader of the free world) and his campaign was very funny. His slogan was "Just a common, ordinary, simple savior of America's destiny."

I eventually settled down and Rachel and I tried to pick up where we left off. But the sands had shifted. I had survived the summer without her, something I thought I could never do. I had become a little angrier, the result of current events. And Rachel became more Jewish. Spending a summer immersed in the culture really rubbed off on her. I guess it could have been worse. She could have come back pregnant.

Still, we pretended nothing changed. Romance resumed in backseat contortion challenges. Do people actually do it on *beds*?

Fall classes were about to start. This time I got smart. I enlisted the help of my mother to run for classes with me. The doors opened at 8:00. We arrived at 6:00. I camped out in front of the class I most wanted. She lined up for the class I second most wanted.

At about 7:45 a girl showed up and joined us in line. To pass the time she had a guitar. She sat on the front steps and sang Joni Mitchell's "Both Sides Now."

I was absolutely entranced.

This was maybe the most spectacular girl I had ever seen. Long silky red/brownish hair, the face of an angel. And a perfect lithe body. Much like when Ann sang "Over The Rainbow" that day in the 7th grade, I fell instantly head-over-heels in love. The song ended, everyone clapped, she acknowledged with a shy smile that, of course, was the most endearing thing you've ever seen.

And then the clock struck eight. The doors opened. There was a mad scramble, and in the rush I lost sight of her.

And never saw her again.

For four years at UCLA I searched for her. I would take different routes to classes. I would frequent distant campus locations and wander through dormitory lobbies. There wasn't a rally or protest I missed, even for causes I didn't give a shit about. One UCLA-USC football game at the Coliseum I trudged up and down the stairs, aisle after aisle, perusing the student section. Nothing. It's like she was a mirage, a vision. But I know she was real. And there wasn't a day on campus, no matter who else I was dating, that I didn't look for her.

It's love's illusions I recall

I really don't know love at all.

Rachel and I split up in September. Our Grassroots concert was Friday night. Much to my surprise, she said she couldn't go. It was the Jewish Sabbath. What??? We had always gone out before on Friday night. But now it was more important to observe the Sabbath. That was the last straw. I certainly respected her beliefs but Jesus! I worked all summer on this goddamn thing! I was used to ceding to her wishes, but not this time. So over the phone I told her maybe it was best we just stopped seeing each other. There was silence. I'm sure she wasn't expecting *that*. Certainly not from me. And I didn't expect her to relent. I knew how intractable she could be – a stone wall (of Jerusalem?). So that was that. We awkwardly wished each other well and I hung up.

I thought I'd be destroyed but I wasn't. The summer separation helped. As did "Both Sides Now Girl." And just maybe I had grown up a little? Nah. It was the summer and "BSN Girl."

But there was no acrimony. A very popular theme in music during that period was " *You ruined my life and now you're going to pay, you lying bitch whore!*" Just a few examples: "96 Tears" (as in "you're going to cry them"), "Hey, Little Girl" (it's all over for you), "I'll Feel a Whole Lot Better" (when you're gone), "Delilah" (Tom Jones kills the ho' in that one), every third Dylan song, and who can ever forget Nilsson's immortal, "You Cheated, You Lied, So Fuck You?"

The other dominant theme was that it was okay to be unattached – in fact, preferable. Songs of personal independence were all the rage. "Different Drum," "I've Got to Be Free," "It Ain't Me, Babe" (Dylan wrote half of these, too), "Don't Bring Me Down," "I'm a Wanderer," "I'm a Drifter," "I'm Free," "Go Where You Wanna Go," "We'll Sing In the Sunshine" – we really bought into these naïve anthems to freedom. Who needs other people? Who needs jobs and houses? Those things just *tied us down, man.* As we got older we realized of course that *we* needed them. Just like every other generation since the beginning of time. Now most are singing, "I'm a Divorcee," "Go Where You Can Afford," and "We'll Sing in the Pre-School."

The Grassroots concert was a big success. None of Zelda Gilroy's security concerns surfaced. Everyone had a good time. We raised a lot of money for whatever that very worthy cause was. And the event helped promote awareness for our station. I'm sure we would have had a lot of new listeners on the way home if anyone could've heard KLA in the car.

The fall quarter began the next Monday. A UCLA requirement was three foreign language classes. I knew from my Herculean struggles in high school Spanish that linguistics was not my strong suit. So I thought I did something really crafty. I had signed up for Hebrew. I figured (a) it would all come back from my days in Hebrew school, and (b) I was dating a Hebrew School teacher.

So I break up with Rachel the week before, the course work is all grammar (which we had never studied at Valley Beth Shalom), and most of the students were Israelis looking for a free A. They pretended to know nothing. "Shay-lom" they would utter haltingly. Who were they kidding? They all had names like Zvee and Yitzak and Ya-akov. By session two I was buried.

Other classes that quarter included Statistics, Poli Sci, and the History of Dating. Imagine my disappointment upon learning the latter was a study of carbon dating and determining the age of ancient trees, not who removed the first bra.

My social life was limited at best. Yes, I was now available and there were 30,000 undergraduate students, but I didn't know any of them. The staff of KLA was small and heavily male oriented. There were two cute girls. One had a boyfriend and the other announced that she "didn't date *disc jockeys*." The last two words were spoken with such distaste you easily could have substituted *necrophilia fetishists*.

I wound up going out a few times with girls from my class at Taft who were also commuting and knew nobody.

Still, I was confident I would find somebody. After all, rebound-love was in the air. John Lennon left his pretty blond wife Cynthia for Japanese artist/Svengali/home and group wrecker Yoko Ono. This was a head scratcher on the level of the meaning of life. And then, as further proof that Camelot was officially dead, former First Lady, Jackie Kennedy married rich Greek shipping magnate/codger Aristotle Onassis in October and just sailed around on his yacht. What is it with hot women and older men who own expensive modes of transportation?

And hey, even Tiny Tim found love.

Tiny Tim was 1968's newest sensation. Armed with a ukulele and a falsetto that opened garage doors, this middle-aged goofball burst upon the scene with an excruciating version of "Tiptoe Through the Tulips" and rose to unimaginable popularity. How do I describe him physically? Picture Howard Stern in a fat suit. You can't say he made it on his looks. Or his music. He sang a repertoire of musty old Tin Pan Alley tunes from the turn of the century. On December 17, 1969 he would marry "Miss Vicki" on *The Tonight Show* and the wedding would draw 40 million viewers. He wrote his own vows, which included a promise not to be "puffed up." (This is what we had to do in the '60s before there was *American Idol* to satisfy our insatiable need for making ass-fun of idiots.)

The Fall of America

My airshifts on KLA were much better that quarter. Saturday and Sunday from 9:00-noon. Sure, no one listened, but at least they were awake. And I never had to play Tiny Tim. (My newsman was Zev Yaroslavsky, who went on to become a prominent Los Angeles County Supervisor.)

Since I was spending so much time on campus, I decided to seek a part-time job in Westwood. Luckily, I found one right away. There was a locally owned record store in Westwood Village called the Warehouse. The owner was thrilled to hire someone with experience as opposed to those "hippie freaks that just want to get high as kites behind the Vikki Carr display!"

I took my first plane flight in mid-October! If I could lose my virginity AND fly in a plane then there was hope that someday I might even experience oral sex. (We would land a man on the moon and the New York Mets would win the World Series first. Hell, the Oakland A's would win several World Series first.) A classmate, Jerry Schultz and I flew up to San Francisco to see the UCLA-Cal football game in Berkeley. We stayed at Jerry's house. Even though the flight lasted maybe one hour, this was unbelievably thrilling. Not so much for Jerry. They lost his suitcase. How could United lose luggage on an L.A.-S.F. commuter flight? So for my first flight I was treated to the *full* experience of commercial air travel.

Haight-Ashbury looked considerably seedier than even the year before. For every Janis Joplin and Jerry Garcia who found inspiration, there appeared to be a hundred other residents who would have been thrilled just to find a coupon for Jack In The Box. If '67 was the *"Summer of Love,"* '68 was the *"Fall of Maybe We Should Start Seeing Other People."*

In November, KLA mobilized all its resources to cover election night. They sent people out to the various campaign headquarters. That *was* the sum total of their resources. I was assigned to the Biltmore Hotel downtown where both Hubert Humphrey's and Senator Allan Cranston's camps were camped. This was very exciting. I had a real press credential and could enter any restricted ballroom and watch volunteers blow up balloons. The presidential race was way too close to call, even hours after the west coast polls closed. So most of the time we media folk just raided buffet tables and schmoozed. One local reporter who was very nice and chatted with me for close to an hour was Channel 4's Tom Brokaw. Who knew that years later we would both write books about the '60s and his would outsell mine by about two million copies?

At around midnight, the senator's race was over and Cranston had won. We gathered in his ballroom for the victory speech. I was standing just off the stage. Cranston entered followed by his staff. His campaign manager was Jess Unruh, rumored to be running for California governor in two years. Unruh was standing right next to me. So after Cranston completed his speech I turned to him, held out my microphone and asked if he was planning to run. He dodged the question, saying it was senator Cranston's night. But I was young and brash and in college and didn't give a shit. I began goading him. "Come on, you know you're going to. What's the big deal? Why can't you just say it? It's not like it's a big secret."

He continued to duck me and eventually slipped away. When I got home late that night there was a message that my aunt from Louisville had called. Apparently my whole exchange with Jess Unruh had been carried live on ABC. I probably got more national exposure that election night than Tom Brokaw.

Jess Unruh did run for governor two years later. He lost.

By the next morning it was official. Richard Milhous Nixon had defeated Hubert Humphrey in one of the closest elections in history. (The closest was when Al Gore actually *won* but George Bush became President.) Nixon vowed to reunite the country. It took years but he succeeded as the entire nation banded together to finally force him out of office.

The convention riot actually helped elect him. Much of the population blamed the melee not on the overzealous authorities but *those disruptive hippies*. Voters wanted law & order. So they elected the man who would, himself break the law.

At the time the voting age was still 21. If 18-year-olds were allowed to vote in 1968, Pat Paulsen would have been this country's 37th President.

Nixon's election victory was yet another nail in the coffin of baby boomer idealism. We start the year with such thrilling new voices as Eugene McCarthy and Robert Kennedy and wind up with Top Cat. The drugs and marijuana we young *long-haired hippie freaks*consumed became less about recreation and more about just coping.

Student rallies were now commonplace at UCLA. I attended them all, but if I'm being honest, I was there as an observer. If I wasn't covering them for KLA I was combing the crowd for "BSN Girl." Not that I wasn't supportive of the "cause" and all, but I wasn't the guy in all those '60s college unrest movies who wanders innocently into a protest and an hour later is burning a bank and sleeping with Mia Farrow. Still, I wasn't on the outside looking in. I was more like on the *inside* looking in.

My grades that quarter were respectable, and by the skin of my teeth I even passed language class. But it is humiliating when a Jew gets worse grades in Beginning Hebrew than a Mormon and a Samoan kid.

Christmas break was spent working twelve hours a day at Warehouse Records. The big seller: The Beatles' *White Album.* In fact, it was the fastest selling album in the history of the music industry. And it was one of the most expensive. Retail stereo albums went for $4.79. This LP (a double album) sold for $11.79. I guess the cost of maharishis, LSD, and British divorces were going up.

The Beatles were really on a roll because their single "Hey, Jude" was the biggest selling single of the year and their biggest selling single *ever.* If only I didn't hate it. It's the only Beatles song I can't stand. And of course, it's the only Beatles song that's seven-minutes long.

Dad's Miline Club holiday show this year was *Cumalot.* I don't remember who he played but I'm sure it was a very tasteful role.

The second week of winter break I came down with a horrendous cold and spent New Year's Eve sneezing and hacking alone in bed watching *Casablanca* for the first time in my life. Finally! A romantic New Year's Eve!

Apostles of Non Violence Racial Harmony... and other Terrorists

By now the "Generation Gap" had been trivialized to where ABC had a prime time game show with that theme. ABC also had *The Mod Squad*, a group of hippie crime fighters.

In 1968, music sales topped 100 million for the first time in history. In 1969 sales of marijuana topped 100 million.

No one knew it at the time, but once in office, Nixon wasted no time. He immediately instituted *Operation Cointelpro* – the escalation of the FBI's secret war on dissent in America. Targets included (quote): *Advocates of new lifestyles and apostles of non-violence racial harmony.*

Meanwhile, some on the left theorized that the hippies were the end result of a plot by the CIA to neutralize the anti-war movement with LSD, turning the protestors into self-absorbed zombies.

Yes, these were insane times but at least all the enemies we were fighting were imaginary.

For me, 1969 meant a new year, new quarter, and new language. Obviously I couldn't make it through two more sessions of Hebrew. Or weeks. And no one said I had to take three quarters of the *same* language. So I switched to Italian.

I had heard it was easy. And it was… until the scandal broke out the second week.

Apparently several teachers' assistants had been sleeping with female students and giving them A's. They tried to justify this by saying it *was* a romance language, but that didn't fly. The result: Obligatory outrage by the department with a vow to make Italian the hardest language in the history of linguistics. By week three I would have slept with the TA's for even just a passing grade.

I also took "Abnormal Psychology," which proved helpful years later in dealing with actors. One of the assignments was to do some inappropriate behavior in public and study everyone's reaction. This seemed stupid to me. You *knew* what their reaction was going to be. Based on the behavior, either anger or discomfort. So I figured, if I'm going to do this pointless exercise I might as well have a little fun with it.

So I put on a jacket and tie, grabbed my trusty broken briefcase, and set out once again to sell Amway products.

Except, this time at 11:00 at night.

Knowing that homeowners would be furious, I figured why go door-to-door and disturb them? I didn't have to repeat this behavior twenty times. I really only had to do it once. So I got in my car, headed to one house in particular, marched up to the front door, and at about 11:30 rang the bell.

Helen's anti-Semite dad answered the door and was practically apoplectic when he saw me. I launched right into my pitch. "Hi, there, Mr. P. Sorry to bother you so late but I'm trying to make as much money as I can. I really love money. And I have two other jobs, because like I said – I *really* love money. So could I show you some miracle products that…?"

I think that's as far as I got. He literally chased me off the property. Mission and assignment accomplished.

One classmate chose to urinate on the front steps of the administration building. He said people just walked by as if it were normal. I always thought as a snapshot of campus life in the late '60s that was the perfect image.

Super Bowls were still no big thing but that was about to change. I didn't watch most of Super Bowl III because it went on at 10:00 AM. in the west and I was busy playing records for nobody on KLA during that time. But I got off the air in time to listen to the end on the radio and be astounded like everybody else. Brash quarterback Joe Namath of the AFL's New York Jets guaranteed they would beat the heavily-favored Baltimore Colts of the powerhouse NFL.

And they did!

16-7 was the final. More important than just bragging rights, the Jets' win established parity for the upstart AFL. Within a few years the two leagues would merge and I don't think that would have ever happened were it not for "Broadway Joe's" stunning upset win.

I couldn't have been more pleased. I always loved these underdog leagues that formed in the '60s – the ABA with their goofy red, white, and blue basketballs, and the AFL. Both leagues emphasized offense so there was always plenty of action. Rarely did you see an NFL game with a final score of 55-49, but in the AFL that was a defensive showdown. And for whatever reason, AFL games always seemed to be played in the absolute worst weather conditions. I think games were canceled if they didn't occur in blizzards and monsoons. A receiver would catch a pass in the driving rain and slide another ten yards in the mud. A player would run laterally five yards out of bounds because he couldn't see the lines of the field in the snow. This was entertaining football! And every year you'd hold your breath that the league wouldn't fold. Now, thanks to Joe Namath, that wasn't going to happen. Thus III ranks second on the list of Super Bowls that had the most impact on society (right behind XXXVIII when Janet Jackson flashed her nipple).

If You Can't Beat Them... Beg Them For a Job

Bob Cohen, who worked at KLA was also a sports intern at another radio station. He told me there was an opening. Weekends from 3:00-11:00 PM. Minimum wage. This sounded perfect. The chance to work at a real radio station! Where do I apply? There was only one very slight problem. It was KMPC. Yes, *that* KMPC. That evil corporate behemoth that wouldn't allow us to broadcast UCLA sports to maybe three listeners.

This was a big moral dilemma. For twelve seconds.

I got in my car and raced down to KMPC and got the job.

Hey, it's not like they murdered puppies.

I couldn't believe my good fortune. I was actually working inside a radio station. And a big one. From the street, their facility on Sunset Boulevard in Hollywood looked like the White House. This was the Taj Mahal of broadcasting.

Many of the personalities were national names. In addition to *Laugh In's* Gary Owens, Wink Martindale and Jim Lange handled shifts between hosting game shows. Roger Carroll was the announcer on the super-cool *Smothers Brothers Show*. Morning man Dick

Whittinghill was an L.A. institution. These weren't disc jockeys. These were *stars*.

Their announcer for the Angels and Rams was Dick Enberg, who went on to become a premiere network sportscaster. Fellow Angel broadcaster Dave Niehaus (later my partner calling Seattle Mariners' games) was inducted into the baseball Hall of Fame in 2008.

The news department included many prestigious former network announcers and former alcoholics. Those AA meetings must've sounded like Orson Welles' dramas.

My job was to write a one-page sports report to be delivered every half hour during newscasts. I also had to keep track of all the scores, change the teletype ribbon, answer phones, and since all of the police monitors were over my desk, I had to alert everyone if there was a bus plunge.

I proudly handed my very first sports report to the great Ben Chandler and turned up the volume to hear it. As he read it I could see him put his hands to his head as if to say, "Oh shit!" Reading exactly what I wrote he said, "In hockey, Montreal leads Detroit 2-0 in the second *quarter*." Hey, it turns out they only play three periods in hockey. Who knew? Certainly not the *sports expert* at KMPC.

The Greatest Goldie Hawn Story Ever

This schedule did not do wonders for my social life. Between my 9:00-noon shift on KLA and KMPC from 3:00-11:00 my weekends were pretty well booked. A couple of the KLA staffers lived in the dorms and invited me to Friday night parties they hosted. Well, they weren't exactly *parties* in the celebration/festive/ fun sense.

We'd sit in someone's dark dorm room. They would put aluminum foil over the windows. They would shine a desk lamp on a Snoopy black light poster. Nine of us would sit on the two lumpy beds that faced each other passing around joints and drinking Red Mountain wine out of coffee mugs. Red Mountain wine came in gallon jugs and maybe cost five bucks but what it lacked in *nuance* it more than made up for in potency. Jimi Hendrix or Cream albums would be playing. No one spoke. We all just nodded and "*got stoned, man.*" No interaction was necessary because we were all into our "*own trips,*" y'see.

My trip was trying to find girls, which was pointless at these opium dorms. Red Mountain was pretty much the wine of losers.

I did meet someone in my "History of Documentary Films" class, though. To this day I have no idea why I took it. Three hours a week of Eskimos freezing to death in 1910 or Nazi propaganda films.

But I met Honoria Feldman. She had the most beautiful olive skin, the most gorgeous blue eyes, and the worst name of any girl I ever dated. In a desperate attempt to stay awake during these interminable exposes of 1937 Russian smelt fishermen, I would mutter snarky comments to my friends within earshot. "Watch. They're going to gut the whale and find twenty elves and a thousand candy canes." Honoria overheard, found me amusing, and that's pretty much how most of my relationships began.

I asked her out to a movie we could stay awake for and she accepted. Honoria was in a sorority so I picked her up at the house. Wow. I had never been in a sorority house before. Sure not like its frat equivalent. There was a lovely main foyer with a chandelier. *A chandelier* for godsakes! Everything was clean. Everything was painted. There was no smell of vomit anywhere. *I* wanted to pledge.

Honoria and I went out for about a month. Things might've worked out much better had it not been for *All My Babies*, a documentary set in the Deep South that was shown in class one day... after lunch. Honoria and I were watching it. I had my arm around her. We were sharing Milk Duds, as only lovers can. A midwife is seen entering some filthy shack. Ho hum ho hum. And then, in the most graphic detail you can possibly imagine, in this absolute squalor, we see a mother give birth. The blood, the ooze, the umbilical cord. This made the abortion scene in *Alfie* seem suitable for "Anything Can Happen Day" on *The Mickey Mouse Club*. As we fled the auditorium, both nauseated, all Honoria could say was "I'm never having babies, NEVER having babies!" and "if you even come near me with that thing I'm CUTTING IT OFF!"

Have you noticed a pattern in the women I dated? Strong-willed and no sex. Honoria had maybe the most rigid personality of all. Early on I casually asked, "Do you go by any nicknames? Honey or something?" "No!" she exclaimed firmly, "My name is *Honoria*!"

Ohhhhh-kay...

(Years later, when I was writing for MASH, we needed a name for Charles Winchester's sister. Honoria Winchester was born. Honoria is pronounced "*Ha-NOR-ee-a*" by the way. But Hawkeye had some fun at Charles' expense by pronouncing it "*Hana-rhea*." This is why you don't want to go out with writers if you take yourself too seriously.)

Honoria was very big on Feminist causes. That was fine but I did get a little tired of hearing how I, by inference, was holding down an entire gender. One major contribution our generation made was in the area of women's rights. No longer was a woman expected to just be Suzy Homemaker. She could enter the workforce. And not just because she knew shorthand or could serve a highball at 30,000 feet. For the first time, women joined the executive ranks, not to mention the police force, military, and Teamsters. (Today, half of law and medical school students are women. 60% of married couples have two incomes. And women are finally beginning to earn the respect they deserve in the workplace, although it's a slow process. Men are learning not to treat them merely as sexual objects one lawsuit at a time.) That said, it's not like I ever asked Honoria to iron a shirt.

What broke us up was this: I took her to a James Brown concert. At the Shrine Auditorium. Downtown. The Big K kingdom. There were maybe 10,000 people in the audience. We were the only two who were white. The show was electric! James Brown truly *was* the hardest working man in show business. Egads, what energy! By the time he (and the Fabulous Flames) did his grand finale, flinging the cape off to wail another chorus of "Please Please," the audience was in an absolute frenzy. I'm sure Honoria would have appreciated the theatrics more if she wasn't terrified. Honestly, and I know this doesn't sound like me, but I never feared for our safety, even for a moment. Something about the vibe in that building, this was not a night for racial differences; this was a celebration of great music and a master showman. There was total unity that evening... except for Ms. Feldman.

Not only did I never see Honoria naked; I actually got farther with Goldie Hawn.

Okay, that *might* possibly require an explanation.

KMPC's Gary Owens arranged for me to watch them make *Laugh In* at the NBC studios in Burbank. They were filming blackout sketches that day – quick sight gags. So there was no audience. Just the cast and crew and me in a big drafty soundstage filled with flimsy sets and props. Very workmanlike and informal. No one even noticed I was there.

On the agenda that day was a series of blackouts featuring 23 year-old Goldie Hawn as a cute little French maid negotiating a mop and bucket. A self-contained kitchen set with two walls was wheeled onto the sound stage.

For one of the gags, Goldie was to plunge her mop in the bucket and water would shoot up into her face. The only problem (besides the gag not being remotely funny) was that the set was on a solid base. There was no way to attach the hose to the bottom of the bucket. So someone had the bright idea that they could just get a thin clear color hose and run it up Goldie's leg and if shot at just the right angle it would appear the geyser of water was sprouting from the bucket.

Ten minutes later, a hose was produced and handed to Goldie. I'm standing right in front of her. She's on this two-foot high base.

She runs this tube up her leg and lifts her little mini skirt to slip it through her panties. But when the drippy hose meets her panties they instantly become invisible.

So there I am – callow, 19-year-old, a mere inches away, standing eye-to-eye with Goldie Hawn's perfectly visible vagina.

Later in the year we would land a man on the moon, perhaps mankind's greatest achievement. I was more in awe of *this*.

These Are the Good Old Days

The latest craze of the decade was remembering the previous decade. '50s nostalgia was *in,* in a big way. We longed for that period before the Vietnam War and social strife when life was simple and innocent and other than the looming threat of total nuclear obliteration, we didn't have a care in the world.

KHJ seized upon this trend to present their most ambitious production to date. On the weekend of February 21-23 they presented the "History of Rock n' Roll" – a 48-hour "rockumentary" tracing the birth and evolution of rock music.

Like all of Los Angeles that rainy weekend, I stayed glued to my radio from noon Friday until its conclusion Sunday night. Today if a station gets a 3 share that's huge. The History of Rock n' Roll scored an astounding 30.6 share that weekend.

Monday morning at KLA everyone was buzzing about it. My concert promoter cohort Tom wondered if someday there would be a nostalgia craze for *this* era? "Over what?" somebody asked. Nothing about the present seemed distinctive or remotely memorable.

(Looking back, *everything* about the period was distinctive. We just never realize it while we're living it. Someday they'll be studying more recent times and waxing nostalgic about piercing tongues, tattoos, and Lady Gaga. And every conversation from every generation about any decade will always end with the same sentence: "What were we *thinkin'*?")

That was assuming there'd a future beyond 1969. And I'm not talking about our old friend nuclear eradication. Dr. Paul Ehrlich wrote a book called *The Population Bomb* in which he prophesized that the population was growing at such an out-of-control rate that by the 1970's the earth will not have enough resources to feed everyone. Wars and mass death will result! What a buzz kill to the Sexual Revolution *this* was. However, there's always a silver lining. The larger the population, the more consumers there are and Dr. Ehrlich sold two million copies of his book. The message seemed a little alarmist to me... except when I was on the freeway.

Another movie spoke to me in 1969 – *Goodbye Columbus*. Adapted from the novella Phillip Roth wrote when he was like eight, this was the tale of a young middle class Jewish man, Neil (Richard Benjamin) falling in love with a wealthy Jewish American Princess, Brenda (Ali McGraw). She was beautiful, headstrong, and initially withheld sex. Brenda turned lovesick Neil into her little bitch. See any connection with me?

Our promotion director at KLA, Sharon Weisz, arranged to get some merchandise and soundtrack albums from *Goodbye Columbus* to give away as contest prizes. So what if KHJ was giving away new cars? We had *Goodbye Columbus* bumper stickers!

I accompanied Sharon to Paramount studios to pick up this coveted crap. It was my first time ever on a real movie studio lot and I was in awe. I would eventually spend fifteen years on the Paramount lot – writing, producing, and directing TV. And when

I'd be stuck in grueling all-night rewrites or getting calls from the network canceling my show I would think back to that day and remind myself of just how lucky I was. Even in the bad times, this was a real Hollywood ending. (Except CBS never should have yanked *Almost Perfect*. God damn it; that was a good show!)

What If God Were One of Us?

Campus unrest continued to escalate. In anticipation of one noon rally, armed storm troopers staked out positions on building roofs. Imagine walking to class, glancing up, and seeing loaded rifles trained on you. It promoted a real collegial atmosphere. And the speaker that day, the militant rebel rouser who Governor Reagan suspected would incite major violence – Candice Bergen.

Here's how touchy things had gotten – riot police were called in to preserve order during a celebration rally. The UCLA Bruin basketball team won its fifth National Championship under coach John Wooden. Led by senior Lew Alcindor (who would go on to become Kareem Abdul Jabbar, thus taking the name before I could), the Bruins beat Purdue 92-72 to win the national title.

UCLA won the national championship all four years I was there. I went from Alcindor my first year to Bill Walton my last. And this will kill you. Know how much tickets were for students to sit right at center court? Twenty-five cents a game. There could be storm troopers beating up kids in the aisles; for that price, I went to every game I could.

When I think of John Wooden I think of that Joan Osbourne

song – "What If God Were One of Us?" The most impressive man I've ever met used to celebrate UCLA victories by joining his wife and another couple at Dolores' coffee shop on Santa Monica Blvd. This was a grungy '50s style diner, one of those 24-hour joints that catered to kids, seedy street people, and lonely souls. No wonder I found myself there after a game one night. Once I discovered that Dolores' was a Coach Wooden ritual, I too went after every game. It was an honor just to be ordering off the same greasy menu as him.

Few have ever led lives as honorable and humble as Coach Wooden. At a time when we were all questioning...well... *everything*, here was a man preaching fundamental humanity. His lessons seemed "old fashioned" and simplistic, but we listened because his basketball teams always won. It was only when we ourselves matured that we realized the lessons were deeply profound and his once-hokey "Pyramid of Success" was in fact a superb game plan for living your life.

I heard a lot of great people speak at UCLA, but none more inspiring and wise than John Wooden. *That* is who we should have been listening to – not some idiot maharishi or drugged-out Harvard professor.

Getting arrested at one of these student rallies was a misdemeanor. I steered clear of that, preferring the more exciting felony crimes.

All of us at KLA were forever frustrated that our signal was so weak that no one could hear it. For all the time and effort we poured into the station it would be nice if we had *some* listeners, even just a few. So we illegally boosted the power, figuring no one would notice. (Sometimes I'm completely floored by how stupid I was.)

For several days it was heaven. You could hear KLA at the airport, in Hollywood, the Valley; pretty much the entire west side.

Then the FCC descended upon us like killer bats. They threatened to pull the plug and worse, lock us all up for twenty years. I almost plotzed.

Not *again.*

This was the second time that *month* I faced life imprisonment. Let me back up:

One of my radio geek pen pals from New York discovered this easy-to-build little box that you could attach to your phone line. When switched on it fooled the phone company into thinking the phone was still ringing. You were able to make long distance calls for free. Back then long distance was a big deal. When you flew somewhere and wanted to alert the folks back home that you had arrived safely, you called them collect asking for yourself. Your loved ones would tell the operator you weren't home, but the message had been received. That's right. There used to be a time when the phone company employed actual live people to provide customer service. These people were called "operators."

Every spare hour I would talk long distance to New York or wherever my fellow lawbreakers were. Unfortunately, one got busted. And it made the front page of the New York Post. I lived in terror that they would trace his calls and catch me as well. Luckily, that never happened. And the phone company realized that to prosecute a teenager who ran his major crime ring from his bedroom in the family home in Long Island would not bring great PR to the company. So the case went away. As did my magic box.

The phone company at the time had a bigger problem on their hands. Captain Crunch cereal was giving away free plastic whistles inside each box. Someone discovered that if you blew the whistle into the telephone receiver it was the same frequency phone repairmen used to make calls without being charged. So for a while, thousands of people from all over were making free long distance calls compliments of the good Captain. Eventually the phone company had to change all its frequencies. It only made $26,999,999,999 in profit that year and not $27,000,000,000.

The FCC ultimately slapped us on the wrists and I beat that rap too. But believe me, I learned my lesson. I was sufficiently "scared straight" from those two incidents to completely walk the straight and narrow from then on. Oh sure, there was the time I was almost deported from Canada but that was in the '70s.

Driving Miss Zsa Zsa

Taking Italian "Pass/Fail" allowed me to barely pass and satisfy the language requirement. But I still speak it worse than the waiters at the Olive Garden. I was not enjoying Psychology so I thought I'd transfer into the Television/Film department. They told me I needed to submit a film or television program that I had made. I said, "Uh, isn't that what I'm supposed to have AFTER I graduate and after you've taught me how to do that?"

Transfer request denied.

Still, I took a lot of television and film courses anyway. I did not take any screenwriting classes, however. Stu Ohman, one of the disc jockeys at KLA had his heart set on becoming a sitcom writer. He took a course and got an A+ for a *That Girl* script he had written. I read it and thought it was a piece of shit. If that's what they were teaching, I wanted no part of it. Stu wound up an accountant.

There was an extra-curricular TV talk show that aired closed-circuit in the dorms. I volunteered to be a gofer. I'd like to say I gravitated towards television because I wanted to expand my horizons, but the truth is the assistant director was the heiress of a major national furniture chain and I had a major crush on her. I so wanted to sleep with her and get a discount on a new dinette set. Alas, "the store was closed" on both accounts.

One of my assignments was to pick up the guests if they didn't wish to drive themselves. First up was Zsa Zsa Gabor. She was an actress/ personality known more for her nine marriages than her stellar film work. She was one of the Gabor sisters (Eva and Magda being the others of course). Her movies were, uh... never mind, just think of Zsa Zsa Gabor as a 50-year-old Hungarian Kim Kardashian. She was appalled that I showed up in a Ford Mustang – like UCLA was going to send a stretch limo for Zsa Zsa Gabor.

We're driving along in silence. Me in the front and she in the back as if she were in a limo. All I needed was the little hat. Finally, I decided to make a little conversation. I asked her what I should do about the furniture heiress. "Vell, get a new car, darlink," was her first suggestion. I don't recall her other tips (probably buy her expensive silverware); I just recall thinking how absurd this was that I was getting love advice from Zsa Zsa Gabor.

My greatest pick up though, was Moe Howard. Holy shit! An actual Stooge was in my car! Sitting in the front seat even! I wish he had poked me in the eyes while driving or threatened to "murderize" me. But he just acted.... *normal*. I might as well have been driving my Uncle Lou who made seat covers. Whereas Zsa Zsa called me "darlink," Moe called me "boychick."

Like most kids of my generation, the Three Stooges were Gods. Their short films were just pre-movie filler in the '30s. But they were the ideal length for inserting between commercials on television in the late '50s. And suddenly these three old knockabout Vaudevillian comics became a national sensation. The fact that this recognition came so late and was so unexpected, I think Moe relished it all the more. He was humble and kind and it was a *shtik naches* (great joy) to meet him. And he said if the furniture heiress didn't like me for who I am I should move on.

In addition to Italian, I also passed my other classes. Not only don't I remember what I learned. I don't even remember what those classes were. I was counting the days until summer.

Tripping

I always wanted to go to New York. I had heard good things. What fascinated me most was the concept of a subway. You didn't need a car. Kids could travel anywhere from anywhere else without having to worry about going "over the hill" (in fact, you were going "*under* the hill"). The city was at their feet! Entire neighborhoods were one block instead of a ten-mile community. And everyone seemed Jewish, even the people who weren't.

Obviously my perception of New York was skewed and somewhat romanticized. There weren't doo wop groups on every street corner, your friends weren't as funny as Woody Allen, and all the girls weren't the Shangri-Las (a singing group of very talented hot sluts). But I had to see it. I had to ride those subways. I had to hear WABC and the great Dan Ingram actually coming out of my transistor radio.

My parents didn't think tapping out my savings account for the second time in two years was such a great idea for a three week adventure, but I reminded my father that this was money I had earned and could do whatever I wanted with it. He nodded and said, "You'll have a great time."

So look out New York, I'm coming! Also, look out Pittsburgh, Washington D.C., and Louisville because you can't go back east without visiting those hot spots too.

The plan was this: Three weeks. First week in Gotham. Then meet-up with one of my radio freak buddies and drive with him to his home in picturesque Pittsburgh. Spend a day or so soaking in the wonders of the Steel City and then fly to D.C. See those sights and stop off in Louisville to visit my cousin Craig on the way home. I had introduced him to the Sunset Strip a couple of years ago. He could return the favor and show me where they filmed some scenes from *Goldfinger*.

And all the airlines offered great deals for students. You could fly for half price. The airlines were all regulated back then; all required to charge the same fares. The carriers all cried that they couldn't make money this way so in the late '70s the government relented and dropped pricing regulations. Within months several long established airlines went bankrupt. But in 1969 fares were standard.

And you could get huge discounts on hotel rooms if you were a student. So for maybe a couple hundred bucks I booked all my flights and reserved a room in New York at the prestigious Statler Hilton across the street from Madison Square Garden for only $9.50 a night.

I checked in my suitcase (for free) and my family escorted me right to the gate. People dressed up to fly on airplanes. (You didn't see one single "SHIT HAPPENS" t-shirt.)

I flew TWA, a major carriers, like United or American. (Now dead because deregulation was a GREAT idea.) Once in the air they distributed free headsets so we could listen to seven channels of music. Moments later, carts were wheeled down the aisles and we were all served a hot breakfast – omelets or French toast. And the utensils were genuine metal! Then a big screen was lowered and they showed a free movie (*Support Your Local Sheriff* with James Garner). But that was nothing. Here's the kicker: I've never seen this on any other flight I've ever taken – they set up a big brunch buffet. We all lined up down the aisle and helped ourselves to lox, bagels, cold cuts, fruit and various salads.

And this was *coach*!

The guys in First Class must've been getting blowjobs.

Landed at JFK around 4:00 and taxied into the city, getting my first look at that Manhattan skyline. Wow! The Doris Day/Rock Hudson movies didn't do it justice. I was Jon Voight in *Midnight Cowboy* – a wide-eyed rube taking in the "big city" for the first time. This was a world unlike any I had ever witnessed. Just the sheer number of WIGS stores was staggering to me. How many New Yorkers needed wigs?

I arrived at my hotel, a grand old structure of stature and grace, and then shown to my elegant $9.50 a night room. It was the size of a litter box. There was one single bed, a window that looked out at the back of the Gimbels' Department Store neon sign, and a TV that was so old it said "the Dumont Network" above channel 5. But I didn't care. I was really in New York. I turned on my transistor radio and there was Dan Ingram on WABC trashing some sponsor's frozen clam dip.

I just walked around that first night. Saw the Empire State Building, Macy's, seventeen WIGS stores. I had dinner at Howard Johnson's. I didn't feel self-conscious that I was eating alone because everyone there was eating alone.

After dinner I wandered into Madison Square Garden. There was a Billy Graham Crusade that week. Billy Graham was a charismatic TV evangelist who rose to great prominence with lavish stage extravaganzas… I mean, *religious services*. But admission was free (donation cups were passed around like joints) so I checked it out. I didn't find God but I did see where the Knicks and Rangers played.

Lying alone in bed that night, my mind drifted back to Bev Fine.

She was living somewhere in New York. I had no idea where or how to get in touch with her. But I began to fantasize. I'd somehow get her number, call her, and she'd be delighted to hear from me. There'd be no "Poconino" chants in the background. She offers to come get me the next day and show me around New York. She arrives, I open the door, and she looks spectacular. We hug and it's an "*Ann in the gym*" moment. She takes me around Manhattan. We ride subways, visit museums, the Statue of Liberty, Central Park, the Village. You've seen this movie montage many times. Sharing an ice cream cone, finding bargains in the street, holding hands at dusk, a romantic dinner at an outdoor café, late night jazz, then back to my room where we make love bathed in the glow of the flashing Gimbels' sign.

Sigh. If only.

Here's what really happened: The next morning, Jonathan (my local radio geek friend) showed me around town. First we hopped on the subway. Tokens were fifteen cents. The subway was everything I imagined. When you're used to freeway traffic the idea of getting in a train and just going was magic to me. In minutes we were in midtown. And it was the first time I had ever seen an abortion clinic ad.

We hit stations WABC, WMCA, WNEW, WHN. If I'm not going to see Central Park and the Statue of Liberty with Bev Fine then they can wait. But watching WABC's Chuck Leonard read live copy for Korvette's department store, *that* I had to see the first day. The world's biggest nerd goes to New York.

For lunch we went to Nathan's in Times Square. The place (which was enormous) was packed. Hundreds of people eating lunch while just standing at raised counters pressed together like sardines. This was Jupiter to me. Sampled my first Nathan's hot dog and the obligatory waffle fries. I always thought Pink's in L.A. was the best (so did Orson Welles who would down two dozen nightly and not coincidentally die). Nathan's was better. Best food I've ever eaten standing.

For the rest of the week I did do the touristy things (all the while imagining what it would have been like seeing them with Bev). Took the Circle Line boat tour around Manhattan (which I highly recommend), saw Rockefeller Center, Central Park, a Mets game at Shea Stadium (what a dump), even ducked into a museum or two. With me always was my trusty transistor radio. "In the Year 2525" by Zager & Evans was the number one song in New York and WABC played it every hour. When I hear it today it brings a nostalgic smile to my face. Then I change the station.

Saw my first Broadway show – *Promises Promises*, the musical adaptation of *The Apartment*. Book by Neil Simon and music by Burt Bacharach & Hal David. It started a half hour late. Mayor Lindsey was coming and they held up the curtain for him. The audience was almost mutinous. I think the test of a good show is if they can win over 600 angry New Yorkers who have babysitters to pay and trains to Long Island to catch. *Promises squared* delivered. (Ten years later I would work with one of the actors. Edward Winters played Colonel Flagg on *MASH*. I asked if he remembered that night. He thought a moment, nodded, and said, "It was a Wednesday, it had rained earlier in that day, someone had brought in a cake for the prop master's birthday and… No! How the fuck am I supposed to remember *that*? We did a jillion shows." I went right back to the office and added five more Colonel Flagg jokes. I loved that guy.)

As I walked back on 8th Avenue at midnight (not knowing any

better) I passed a phone booth. The Bev Fine fantasy kept running through my head. So at the minuscule chance I might get lucky I ducked into it and opened the thick phone directory. Maybe she had her own phone line. Or seeing the names would jog my memory and I'd remember her dad's name. There must've been a thousand Fines. Page after page. No *Bev*, no *Beverly*, about 200 *B's* if I wanted to just start cold calling, and no father names jumped out. I knew going in it was a real Hail Mary, but that didn't lessen my disappointment. I slunk out of the booth and headed back to my hotel longing for someone I knew was now out of my life.

Greenwich Village was my next night's destination. I wanted to see Bob Dylan but the timing wasn't right. Apparently I missed him by two days and seven years. But that Bohemian sense of vibrancy and discovery was still alive. Everywhere you looked there were nightclubs, experimental theaters, used bookstores, record stores, and galleries. Street musicians filled Washington Square. It was Haight-Ashbury for people looking to stimulate their minds, not fry them. This was one of those "anything is possible" places. Well, *almost* anything. Bev was not in any of the clubs or coffee houses. "Stop it!" I kept telling myself.

All I remember about Pittsburgh is this: My other radio buddy, Ken J. and I arrived at his family home late at night after an exciting journey on the Pennsylvania turnpike. The guest room where I slept was in the basement. At 7:00 the next morning a phone in the room rang loudly. I woke up startled, my eyes flew open, and the room was pitch black. For maybe twenty seconds I had absolutely no idea where I was. You can't imagine how terrifying that is. It was like my own nightmarish mini LSD bad trip. Along with those cautionary high school films on the dangers of sex, alcohol, and drugs they need to add one about waking up in Pittsburgh.

In Washington D.C. I took all the tours and saw all the sights. This is why you stay awake during U.S. History. These are not just tourist *attraction*s. These are the symbols of a proud heritage. Even in its then-tarnished state. Another big thanks to Mr. Solkovits.

In Louisville, I ate fried chicken.

We Did It!!

There was even more reason to feel pride at being an American later that summer. We landed a man on the moon. Even Walter Cronkite choked up on CBS reporting it. The weekend of July 20th the entire nation was glued to their televisions. President Kennedy's pledge in 1961 that we would land a man on the moon by the end of the decade was about to take place. This was even bigger than "The History of Rock n' Roll."

As when JFK was assassinated, everybody remembers where they were at this moment. I watched at home in Woodland Hills with my family and grandparents. *Taxi* actress, Marilu Henner was busy losing her virginity standing up in the shower.

Americans had become used to space coverage in the '60s. There was really nothing to see: shots of Mission Control in Houston, maps, and anchors at desks. We would hear the communication between Houston and the astronauts. By the Apollo missions, we sometimes got to see live fuzzy video of the crew, usually only for a few seconds. Still, the first time I saw a grainy astronaut let go of an apple and it remained suspended in mid-air I was enthralled. Forget action movies and spectacular stunts. Here was an apple bobbing up and down in outer space. That trick still kills me.

What I do know is this: 450 million people around the world watched Neil Armstrong step onto the moon. And they all saw it at the same time. For the first time in history the entire planet shared a monumental moment together. A moment of awe and disbelief. All the hardships of the world, the various wars, famines, poverty, social injustice, discrimination—they were all put on hold, as if God pushed a pause button. What was more profound – man setting foot on the moon, or that moment of absolute global unity?

And Neil Armstrong – what a great line to mark the occasion: *"That's one small step for man, one giant leap for mankind."* He wanted to say *"one small step for A man"* but inadvertently left out the "A." It does sorta make more sense that way. But still, as a memorable line, it sure has more punch than – *"THIS is American Idol!"*

Grampy Sid had tears in his eyes. He was a teenager when he first heard that some huckleberries in Dayton, Ohio invented a contraption that actually flew in the air. And to go from that to a man landing on the moon all in his lifetime was completely overwhelming.

And it's an even *greater* accomplishment than we realized at the time. The more sophisticated our computers have become the more we've begun to appreciate just how rudimentary and archaic the data and technology was back then. What we thought was state-of-the-art in 1969 was really *the Flintstones build a rocket ship*. And we blasted three human beings into outer space in that thing. Yikes!

The rest of the summer I spent working weekends at KMPC. In those days there were no baseball games on Sunday night so once they all were completed I could write up six sports reports and go home at 6:00 instead of 11:00.

Instead, I asked the newsman on duty, Bruce Anson, if I could write some news stories. I thought, "why not take advantage of this opportunity?" Not that I ever wanted to become a news writer but the more skills, the more doors would be open to me in broadcasting.

Bruce graciously agreed to mentor me. We got the news from two major services, Associated Press and United Press International. The stories arrived via Teletype machines – think player pianos but with typewriters. The copy was very dry so the newscasters would rewrite and improve it. Bruce would hand me a story and say, "Make it sing." I'd bang out my version, give it to him to look over, and he would hand it back with notes for a second draft.

Bruce was a tough taskmaster. "You used five words when you could have used one." "Isn't there a more colorful verb than this? "What exactly are you trying to say?"

One story I wrestled with draft after draft was the Ted Kennedy incident. On July 8th, 37-year-old Senator Ted Kennedy (younger brother of John & Bobby) drove off a bridge and his car plunged into the water off Chappaquiddick Island. He escaped but his passenger, a young woman named Mary Jo Kopechne did not and lost her life. Kennedy compounded the offense by fleeing the scene. It was a national scandal that eventually died down.

(A few years later, Volkswagen had an ad campaign boasting the fact that their cars could float. *The National Lampoon* magazine did a take-off of the ad showing a VW bobbing in water with the tagline: "If Ted Kennedy drove a Volkswagen, he'd be President today." Some were outraged, many amused, but I think all agreed that the ad was right.)

I must've done eight drafts of that story.

Between Bruce Anson's notes and examples, I can honestly say I learned more about writing from him than all my high school and college English teachers combined.

Finally, in September, a house fire story I wrote was delivered on the air as written. I rank that achievement up there with my Emmy.

On the other hand, I was almost fired that August. The sports director was Steve Bailey, but he was really Lou Grant from *The Mary Tyler Moore Show*. He rarely spoke to me and when he did it was only in the form of a grunt. KMPC carried the Rams, and in late summer they played a few exhibition games on Saturday nights. This one Saturday they were down in San Diego. I was barraged with scores – all the baseball games, NFL pre-season action, and a few college football games that got underway early. I felt like Lucy and Ethel in the chocolate factory when the candies kept coming down the conveyor belt faster and faster. Mr. Bailey would call from the stadium every five minutes asking for updated scores.

So much was going on that I couldn't take a dinner break. So I ate some nutritious Chicken Delight fried chicken at my desk. Mr. Bailey calls, I answer, and as I start to update him a chicken bone gets caught in my throat. I can't breathe. I try to cough it up, but nothing's happening. I'm turning blue, starting to swoon. Finally, at the last moment I dislodge it. All the while, Bailey's on the other end barking at me for the scores. "Where are they? Where are they?"

Well, I just snapped.

I screamed into the phone. "HEY, I WAS CHOKING, OKAY?! I ALMOST DIED! WHO GIVE S A FUCK ABOUT THE SCORES!? IT'S EXHIBITION FOOTBALL! OH NO! I'M A QUARTER BEHIND ON THE BROWNS-FALCONS GAME IN DIPSHIT, GEORGIA! IT'S MEANINGLESS! NO ONE FUCKING CARES! THE PLAYERS THEMSELVES DON'T FUCKING CARE! YOU'LL GET YOUR SCORES WHEN I HAVE THEM! AND IT'S HORSESHIT THAT THE DINKY UCLA RADIO STATION CAN'T ALSO CALL THE GAMES!

I hung up and thought, oh shit, I am soooo fired. That's the only time in my life I ever screamed at a superior. I must have been completely out of my mind. Sure enough, 11:00, I'm getting ready to leave and the phone rings. It's Bailey. Much to my shock and relief he apologized. I couldn't believe it. Hey, *I* would have fired me.

But not only did I keep my job, in true Lou Grant fashion, Bailey was impressed that I stood up to him. He appreciated my moxie (what it really was was gross insubordination). From then on we became close. In ten years he would even let me call him Steve and not Mr. Bailey. (I stayed friends with him the rest of his life, and on several occasions brought him in to be one of the guys sitting around the bar at *Cheers*.)

So to review my employment history so far – one company tried to sue me, I almost got one boss killed, and screamed at another. At this rate I figured to be drummed out of the workforce by 22. It proved to be just the opposite. Late that summer I was offered a job for $50,000 a year. At KMPC I was making $2,080 a year.

I declined the offer.

Gary Owens showed some of the comedy material I wrote for him to George Schlatter, the producer of *Laugh-In*. He liked it and offered me a job writing for the show. The only problem was it was full-time. I would have had to drop out of UCLA. And if I did that I would lose my 2S deferment and before you could say "you bet your bippy" I'd be drafted and on my way to Vietnam. So although it killed me – I mean KILLED me – I had to turn down the job.

Helter Skelter

I was working the sports desk in the newsroom on Sunday, August 10th when the Teletype machine started going nuts. Bells were ringing incessantly. Clearly a major story was coming over the wires.

The bodies of actress Sharon Tate, noted hair stylist Jay Sebring, coffee heiress Abigal Folger, and two others were brutally murdered and slaughtered in a Benedict Canyon home. Tate was 8 1/2 months pregnant at the time. Words like "pig" were scrawled on the walls in the victims' blood. For all the violence this country had endured over the decade, nothing was this shocking, this inhumane, this unspeakable.

The following night a second grisly mass murder would be discovered in the Los Feliz district. Leno & Rosemary LaBianca were tied up and stabbed repeatedly. "Rise," "Death to pigs," and "Healter Skelter" were written on the walls in their blood. (Big shock that mass murderers can't spell.)

Astoundingly, at first the police didn't tie the two incidents together. I guess it was just a coincidence there were two unfathomably horrific murder scenes, each with words scrawled at the scene in blood… and in some cases the identical words.

Eventually they did see the connection and several days later arrested Charles Manson and members of his "Family," the cult who committed these ghastly murders. Except, that's not why they were arrested. They were apprehended for a major "auto theft ring." It was only when they were in custody and one of the Family members, Susan Atkins, bragged to fellow cellmates that she killed Sharon Tate did L.A.'s Finest finally crack the case. The other "Family" members not already in custody were rounded up and eventually they would all be found guilty and sent to prison for the rest of their miserable, worthless lives.

Once again the nation was rocked by another senseless violent act. Especially in L.A. First the Watts riots, then the RFK assassination, and now this. How far we had come in such a short time since the Frank Sinatra Jr. kidnapping.

Charles Manson essentially put an end to the hippie movement. The whole perception of "love and peace" became distorted as the population lumped the Manson Family with the rest of the hippie movement.

The phones at KMPC were ringing off the hook. Other stations around the country hoping we could file a report for their newscasts. "From Los Angeles, this is Bruce Anson, KILT news." "From Los Angeles, this is Bruce Anson, KMOX news."

Since so many were calling, our scrambling newsmen didn't have time to accommodate them all. So they let me. With my highish voice and inexperience on the air I must've sounded awful. I can imagine listeners in New York saying, "WMCA has a news correspondent who's nine?"

So what did we do to take our minds off these macabre times? We obsessed over whether Paul McCartney was really dead. A bizarre rumor spread that the Beatle had 'secretly' died in a car accident and had been replaced in the group by an impostor. And there were symbolic *clues* to this truth hidden in the artwork and graphics on the Beatles' albums. Also there were cryptic audio clues hidden in the music itself. Supposedly, if you play Revolution 9 backwards you hear "Turn me on, dead man." At the very end of Strawberry Fields Forever you faintly hear "I buried Paul" (the words were actually "Cranberry Sauce" so you can easily see the confusion).

Paul eventually showed himself in public, which effectively doused the rumors… although I'm sure there are still some who think the guy who's been passing himself off as Paul McCartney the last forty years is just a fake. Back in the '60s we never let the truth get in the way of a good conspiracy.

Help Me Rhonda

I started going out with Rhonda. She lived in Philadelphia and was just out here staying with relatives, one of whom was my friend, Jay. Might this be one of those "summer romances" where you meet, fall madly in love, she goes home in September, you're heartbroken, you remember her always, and she forgets you the minute she enters the jet way? She injures you like no woman ever has, but so what? You got laid!

For date number one, I suggested we see *Easy Rider*, a movie that had been getting a lot of buzz. The saga of two hippies (starring Peter Fonda and Dennis Hopper) traveling across America had struck a real chord. The ending where rednecks shoot and kill them stunned and startled young audiences. (Sorry. SPOILER ALERT.) It was the one must-see movie of the summer. But Rhonda had no interest. So we saw her choice instead—*Chitty-Chitty Bang Bang*, starring Dick Van Dyke.

I got a goodnight kiss.

Since I knew that time was of the essence I decided to just pull out the stops for date number two. I offered to take her to Disneyland. That should be good for at least some hands-inside-the-sweater action. She didn't want to go to Disneyland. She had already been there.

But she did want to go to Japanese Village and Deer Park. What the fuck?!

L.A. had a number of animal-themed attractions back then. Jungleland was way out in Thousand Oaks. The most bizarre was Lion Country Safari. You'd drive around slowly while jungle animals roamed freely around you. Good idea to keep your windows rolled up so the lions wouldn't stick their heads in your car and eat your children.

In Buena Park, not far from Disneyland, was Japanese Village and Deer Park. This featured a Japanese-themed, tranquil, Zen-like atmosphere with gardens and koi ponds, and a teahouse, and dove pavilion. Deer were allowed to wander. You can't believe how crushingly boring this place was.

Another goodnight kiss.

For date number three I suggested Lion Country Safari figuring I would cruise by the lions real slow during mealtime and roll down the window on Rhonda's side of the car. But she wasn't interested so there was no date number three.

Woodstock

One week after the Manson murders, Woodstock took place. 500,000 people attended this three-day music festival in upstate New York. If everyone who *said* they attended actually *did* attend that number would climb to 30,000,000. Like most people, I experienced Woodstock a year later when I watched Martin Scorsese's documentary on the event. On that weekend itself, I caught three-minute tiny glimpses on the evening news. I remember thinking, "Wow, my generation sure does like to get together, doesn't it?" Marches, protests, rallies, love-ins, music festivals—we were nothing if not social.

Woodstock was promoted as "3 Days of Peace & Music." The organizers put together an impressive bill of 32 major acts. In their wildest dreams they had no idea the response would be so overwhelming. Nor could they have predicted the diversity of the crowd – all ethnicities, age groups, religions, and class structures; bonded by rejection of current institutions and society, the desire for a new world order, and free dope. The festival took on a life and magnitude of its own. Many consider Woodstock the pinnacle of the '60s, and perhaps it was. But like I said, the vast majority of us only heard about it or caught the story on the news following the report on new leads in the Sharon Tate slaying.

Still, it must've been truly amazing to have been there. Because to endure the pouring rain (five inches during one three-hour period), mud, lack of bathrooms, gridlock traffic, inevitable hangovers, poor sight lines, sleep deprivation, confusion, hunger, stench, and Swami Satchidananda, that had to be one hell of a swingin' party. There was one doctor for approximately 22,000 attendees, which is about the current ratio in Maui.

After seeing the movie a year later I can honestly say I wish I were there... for some of it. Wish I could have seen Janis Joplin, and all the nudity, and Jimi Hendrix. Yep. That about covers it.

The flip side of Woodstock came on December 6th, when a free Rolling Stones concert at Altamont, California resulted in tragedy as a black man was stabbed to death by a member of the Hells Angels motorcycle gang. Security couldn't be called because, well... the Hells Angels *were* the Security.

Rock music continued to evolve in a much harder-edged fashion. Rock stars like Jim Morrison of the Doors were drawn to the dark side. In much the same way that gurus rose to prominence, Anton LaVey gained a large following among rock stars, occultists, and airhead Hollywood celebrities. LeVay, a former lion tamer and police photographer, became the founder and High Priest of the First Church of Satan, dressing in a devil costume. He once appeared on *The Tonight Show* with Johnny Carson and Roman Polankski cast him as the devil in *Rosemary's Baby*. Years later he had a child who he named Satan Xerxes Carnacki LaVey. (Giving children bizarre names was not uncommon. Frank Zappa named his two little darlings Dweezil and Moon Unit. Good luck finding souvenir coffee mugs and license plates with *those* monikers.)

So the radio airwaves were filled with loud piercing electric guitars. And yet, the number one song of the summer (and the whole year in fact) was "Sugar Sugar" by the Archies – an infectious bubblegum trifle performed by a collection of studio musicians. Okay, shoot me – I liked it, too.

And that worried me. It's the same kind of song I liked when I was twelve. Nagging thoughts began creeping into my psyche that I wasn't maturing as much as I should be. This was nothing new. I was always out of sync. But now I was 19. At what point would I officially become an *adult*? And how would I know? It's not like there's a California State Aptitude test.

I thought when I first had sex that would do it. But apparently it didn't because I still liked bubblegum music, *Gidget*, and malted milkshakes over malted liquor. World events and politics had made me more cynical, but I don't consider that *developmental progress*.

And yet, who knows? Maybe I was being too tough on myself. Maybe I had evolved more than I realized. But again, how would I know? ("In the category of *maturity*, the State of California has determined you to be in the 53rd percentile." "Is that good?" "No. That's only 2 percentage points higher than adolescents who are still carrying around their *blankees*.")

These were indeed "confusing times."

Woody

The movies we were flocking to in summer '69 were decidedly depressing. This seemed to be the new trend, launched by *Bonnie & Clyde*. The heroes died (as they seemed to do in real life). Finally saw *Easy Rider* where Fonda & Hopper are shot for entering a Red State. (Sorry... SPOILER ALERT) *Easy Rider* grossed an astonishing $50 million in 1969. This was the feel-good movie of the year in Georgia.

Midnight Cowboy was the film of the year. Dustin Hoffman as Ratso Rizzo succumbs to disease and dies on a bus to Miami (when the driver is informed, he says there's nothing he can do and continues on to Florida – thus turning the film into a metaphor for Jewish retirement).

By comparison, *Last Summer* was uplifting. A young teenager is raped, but at least she survives. And this is what we were seeing in Drive-Ins on date nights. *Last Summer* was notable for me because a very young nubile Barbara Hershey appeared in the film topless for a few scenes. Imagine what *that* looked like on a screen the size of an airplane hanger.

Not only were these not happy times; we were willing to

pay *money* to be reminded of it.

The James Bond inspired "spy craze" was winding down considerably. Sean Connery left the franchise and for *On Her Majesty's Secret Service*, he was replaced by male model George Lazenby. That's like replacing Harrison Ford as Indiana Jones with Carson Daly. Also, the British import TV show *The Avengers* (a fun spy romp featuring the very sexy Diana Riggs) ended its run that fall. *The Man From U.NC.L.E.* and *Secret Agent Man* both were defeated by the dastardliest doomsday weapon of them all – the Nielson rating box. And *Matt Helm's* Dean Martin went from secret agent to the logical next step – variety show host.

All of these bleak, dreary movies were depressing but tolerable. Television comedy, on the other hand, made you want to get "ol' Betsy" off the wall and put one right between your eyes. *The Brady Bunch* and *Hee Haw* premiered. If this is what people were watching, I obviously had no idea what was funny.

Thank God for *Take The Money And Run*.

As classes resumed in September, I took some forgettable date to the Regent Theater in Westwood to see Woody Allen's new movie, *Take The Money And Run*. I never laughed so much and so hard in my life. Movie comedies at the time were *Dr. Goodfoot And The Girl Bombs* or *The Computer Wore Tennis Shoes*. *Bob & Carol & Ted & Alice* came out that year, but that was more titillation and social commentary than comedy. *Take The Money And Run* was just balls-out funny!

Woody Allen became my idol, savior, guru, and I guess rabbi. In an era where young people were desperately searching for role models—leaders who could inspire them to create a better world, eliminate social injustice, and transcend the human condition; I was following a man who did sight gags with Groucho glasses.

And there was something else in this film that was totally

groundbreaking – the nebbish got the girl! Someone once described the Tom Cruise movie *Top Gun* as a teenage boy's masturbatory fantasy. Well, *Take The Money And Run* was mine. There was hope for us neurotic, bespectacled nerds who couldn't throw a spiral! Sure, you'd have to write the movie *yourself*, star in it, and pay a beautiful actress to play your love interest but still, this was progress!

I quit KLA that quarter. There had been a coup over the summer and the new general manager wanted to take the station in a new direction – playing the cool albums he and his junta liked. No longer would the emphasis be on professionalism and preparation for a career in commercial broadcasting. Now it was some guy playing sitar albums for three hours. I tried it for a couple of weeks using the name Johnny Lizard, but after segueing a cut from "*The Eighty-six Years of Eubie Blake*" into "*Music to Moog By*" I concluded this format was not for me.

The World Series that year figured to be a rematch of the Super Bowl. The heavily favored team from Baltimore (the Orioles) facing the unlikely challengers from New York (the Mets).

The New York Mets were a National League expansion team formed back in 1962. Their roster was made up of castoffs from all the other teams. They weren't just bad. Their first season, they were *end-of-the-world* bad. They lost a staggering 120 games. And it could have been worse. There was a game rained out that was never completed. The Mets never finished better than ninth nor won more than 73 games for their first eight inglorious seasons. And then they won the World Series.

The final game was on a Thursday afternoon and I ditched school to watch it. By now everyone in the country was rooting for the "Amazin' Mets." It was the Cinderella story of the ages. For all the turbulence of the late '60s, there were also some incredible highs. We were either attending funerals or ticker tape parades.

For Better, Four Worse

As more and more young men were being drafted and shipped off to Vietnam there was a growing sentiment that on top of everything else, the draft was discriminatory. Low-education, low-income, underprivileged members of society were getting called to duty in far greater numbers than middle-class kids who could hide out in college, afford good draft lawyers, or pay for hookers to entrap senators. So in the interest of "fairness," the Selective Service System instituted a lottery in 1969. No more 2S college deferments. A random drawing was held and you were assigned a number based on your birthday. If you were one of the first 195 birthdays called, you were drafted. The rest were off the hook.

The first draft was held on December 1st. It was very high tech. Numbers were written on scraps of paper, inserted into capsules, and placed in a shoebox. The shoebox was shaken to mix up the numbers and then someone just reached in and pulled out the capsules. I'm not making this up.

The night of the lottery, I was home in Woodland Hills watching nervously with my family. I figured I had about a 45% chance of beating the rap; those were pretty good odds.

They started calling numbers. You think the results show on *Dancing With the Stars* is suspenseful? In many cases your life literally depended on how you fared this night.

September 14th was selected first. Those poor bastards. Then April 24th, December 30th, and February 14th.

February 14th? Shit!! THAT'S ME!! Out of 366 numbers, mine was chosen 4th. (My brother Corey, who was too young to be eligible, placed 366th). I was hit by a stun gun. Suddenly Vietnam was no longer just a peripheral issue to be discussed at Gomi's and protested at coed-populated rallies. It was real. *My* time to face it.

Dad took me out to the Jolly Roger for a drink (well, several) and did his best to assure me that there were options and we would work something out. At the time I was so self-absorbed in my own plight that it never occurred to me the pain he must've been in. The prospects of a son going off to war. But he didn't have the luxury to feel sorry for himself. He had to put on a good face to console me. When it comes to parents, *that* lottery I absolutely won.

The Selective Service lottery produced new and more creative ways to duck the draft. Running off to Canada was so *1967*. Claiming you were a Conscientious Objector was producing yawns. As was feigning homosexuality. One of my KLA chums came up with easily the most innovative dodge. He had his birthday changed. He was born in a small village in England. He had his mother fly over there, tell the registrar that the birth certificate had been in error and this was her first chance to rectify the problem. So the date was officially changed, this friend re-registered with the draft board and his lottery number went from 48 to 309.

This person, by the way, grew up to become a right-wing reactionary talk-show host advocating the reinstatement of the draft and proposing there be no loopholes for escaping service. Yes, this person is pond scum.

A more honorable way of getting around the draft was to sign up for the Army Reserves. That's what I did the following year. The good news – I stayed out of Southeast Asia. The bad news – it was a six year commitment and I had to keep my sideburns trimmed.

The Return of Rachel

"It's not worth a thousand dollars to get rid of you." That's what my father said when I asked if I could live in the dorms. Room and three meals a day for an entire year for a thousand bucks was still a pretty good deal but not when the alternative was "free and just commute." If I hadn't spent all my savings on the New York trip and taking Rhonda to that goddamn Japanese Village and Deer Park I would have paid for it myself, and in fact, the following year that's just what I did. (See sequel if there is one.)

Even *I* wanted my independence. That New York trip was the first time I was ever out on my own and I quite liked it. I also liked those Friday night dorm parties where I smoked dope and drank cheap wine. A) I could hardly do that in my room at home, and B) I wanted to expand that activity to Saturday… and maybe Sunday-Thursday.

When we say we need to break away from our parents, is that something embedded in our DNA code, or is it really just that we all want to get wasted without having to deal with any shit?

So I was not able to make a clean break that year, but I did exert my independence. In an act of blatant defiance, I got my own telephone. Paid for it myself. Very few kids had their own phones. In fact, in 1969 only 90% of homes even *had* a phone. Not a "smart phone"; *any* phone. There was the family number and maybe some "extensions." I still remember our number. Diamond 87992. (No area code. Today in Southern California there are seven.) But we kids rarely had our own dedicated lines. I think service cost an outrageous ten dollars a month. Still, it was worth it to me to have even a little privacy.

A quick word about phone service. There were many local phone companies in the '60s, but they all were owned by AT&T. In some circles that might be considered a monopoly. And, for good measure, they owned the actual phones, not you. You ordered a phone, a guy with his butt crack showing installed it right into the wall and if you dropped service or moved, the guy waddled back and took the phone away. But I will say this: those telephones were indestructible. You could throw them against walls, pour hot coffee on them, drop them from the Empire State Building—they'd continue to work for fifty years. And then Ma Bell was split up in 1984, customers could finally own their own phones, and suddenly they broke in eleven minutes.

My grades were acceptable that quarter. I even got an A. Okay, it was in Children's Literature but still, there are layers to Winnie the Pooh.

Dad's Miline Club holiday show that year was *Diddler On The Roof.* He played Motel, an actual man. I think he found it harder to play Jewish Orthodox than a woman. After that triumph, my parents went off on a two-week Caribbean cruise, telling my brother and I that Babette was in charge.

I swung by the new post office to mail off Christmas cards to my KMPC co-workers. I'm sure Wink Martindale opened my card and said, "Do I know this person?" The post office and an adjacent

Denny's now stand where the little Fun Land amusement park used to be on Topanga Canyon. Of course, riding that rickety Ferris Wheel and eating at Denny's has the same effect on your stomach.

There, in line, was Rachel. I was a little taken aback. So was she. This was our first encounter in over a year. The first moment was awkward but passed. It was clear we both were glad to see each other. Rachel looked great. The year away from me did not send her into a collision course with ruin. We stood and talked for about fifteen minutes. We probably would have gotten something to eat if there was a decent place nearby.

Catching up, I learned she had relaxed her stance on Judaism and was not seeing anyone at the moment. My stance on Judaism remained relaxed and I wasn't seeing anyone either. I suppose I could have asked her out but I didn't. Not exactly sure why. Had we drifted too far apart? Was I too afraid of rejection? In any event, I skirted the subject.

I kidded her about the upcoming New Year's Eve. Were she and her Camp Ramah buddies going to break into Zody's department store where they had a big bed sale? No, she laughed. The Camp Ramah crowd broke up. (So much for Jewish "tradition"!) She was going to Zorba the Greek's to folk dance on New Year's Eve.

We hugged goodbye with promises to keep in better touch. I drove away knowing that there was still a spark. For both of us.

On Christmas Eve, Corey and I went to Disneyland. This is a secret only Jews know: Disneyland is empty on Christmas Eve. Practically all Christians are preparing for the big day so the park is wide open. No lines for anything. And when they have the big Christmas parade down Main Street there's maybe twelve people watching it. In 24 hours they'll be hanging on the light poles, but on December 24, the Magic Kingdom was ours.

I couldn't get Rachel out of my mind. I'm sure being at Disneyland, where I was obsessed with her the last time I was there, didn't help. Did I want to get back together? Did I still have strong feeling for her or did I just miss the comfort and familiarity of being in a relationship? God, where was Zsa Zsa Gabor when I needed her?

The End of the '60s

It's hard to pinpoint just when the '60s actually "ended." Some think it was when the Vietnam "Police Action" ended but that was in 1975 – we're talking a decade and a half. This book would be longer than *Anna Karenina*. Others believe it was when the Beatles broke up. But there's not even agreement among the Beatles on what date that was. They were each off doing individual projects in 1968 and the exact decision to call it quits as a group could have been made anytime from 1968 through 1970 (although probably 1969 when Paul died).

Was the assassination of Martin Luther King Jr. the end? Or Robert Kennedy? That puts it in 1968. If you go by rock star overdoses then 1970 is the year (Jim Morrison, Jimi Hendrix, Janis Joplin). If you're talking the end of our childhood – 1966, when Walt Disney died.

On the calendar, the '60s ended at midnight on December 31, 1969.

I had no plans for that evening. Corey was off celebrating with friends (read: heavy drinking). My "sister" Terry had a boyfriend. The night was unseasonably cold, even for Los Angeles. Lows were in the 30's. There were frost warnings. Those people camping out in Pasadena, waiting for the Rose Parade, sleeping on the sidewalk were nuts. It's on *TV!* In *color!*

I decided to see *Butch Cassidy and the Sundance Kid* at the Holiday Theater on Topanga. More accurately, I decided to see Katherine Ross who happened to *be* in *Butch Cassidy and the Sundance Kid.* Katherine was yet another reminder of Rachel. They looked similar… to me… then. The movie ended around 10:00. Now what to do?

I hopped in my yellow Mustang, turned on Victory Blvd. and headed east – not so coincidentally in the direction of Zorba the Greek's. Unlike the Bev Fine-New York fantasy, this scenario would most likely be realized: I walk in unannounced. Rachel spots me. She's surprised and delighted. I join the dance line and take her hand. She squeezes it. We look into each other's eyes. And not a word needs to be said. (It's a classic movie moment. Too bad instead of swelling romantic music we get some busy Greek fun stomp.) And after a year of going there and clomping around on Saturday nights while getting virtually nowhere, this time – with just a mere appearance – I can almost guarantee that there will be the full *fireworks extravaganza* as the clock strikes twelve.

But I couldn't do it.

I drove right past.

Maybe because it *was* New Year's Eve. Or *Butch Cassidy*. Its theme that "the world is forever changing" really hit home on this frigid night. Tooling down Victory, past Tampa Ave. and Reseda Blvd. my focus was on the future, and somewhere deep down in my subconscious it just felt wrong to enter a new decade, a whole new chapter of my life, by going back and trying to recapture a high school romance. So for me the '60s ended as I crossed the light at White Oak Avenue at 10:45 on December 31, 1969.

I turned on Balboa Avenue and headed to Bob's Big Boy. Who needs champagne when I could have a Big Boy Combo?

I sat alone in a small booth in the center of the restaurant. It was crowded, mostly with groups of four to eight. I just observed and listened. Nothing said was particularly memorable, but there were amusing lines sprinkled throughout (practically none of them intended). There was a group of high school jocks. I tried to be in that group once. Seems you need coordination. There was a couple with a child. I always projected what that would have been like if Rachel and I had gotten married. Clearly, I wasn't ready. Some college kids were discussing politics – well, *they* thought they were having a discussion; they really were just spouting rhetoric. I *care* but I'm still way too *brainwashed by the bourgeoisie plastic Military-Industrial Complex* to fit into that little conclave. I didn't identify with long-haired shaggy hippies in the corner who were either Crosby, Stills, & Nash or homeless people. I wasn't cut out to be a musician or take the drugs necessary to think that I was one.

I had tried on a lot of hats in the '60s and none of them seemed to fit. You'd think I'd be a little depressed or feel a sense of alienation. *I* would have thought that's what I thought. But strangely, I didn't. I didn't feel isolated, ignored, unaccepted. I was fine. In truth, I felt a sense of contentment. I was thoroughly enjoying myself. Taking in the conversations around me, processing the scene, formulating my opinions on it – that was my "bag," my "trip," my "thing." Now all I had to do was somehow turn that into a marketable skill. But hey, that's what the '70s are for.

The clock struck twelve. Everyone cheered. I raised my glass. On to the new decade! On to adulthood! I took a swig of my Vanilla Shake.

THE END

ACKNOWLEDGEMENTS

I know I also dedicated the book to them, but first and foremost I must thank my parents, Marilyn & Clifford Levine. Through their love and guidance I had a childhood worth writing about. And to Corey—I can't imagine a better brother to go through it with. Love you, bro!

My own family provided constant inspiration and support. Thank you Matt, Annie, and especially my wife, Debby who is my biggest fan and most honest critic.

Blair Richwood is an extraordinary editor. Her objectivity, insight, expertise, and imagination turned my manuscript into an actual book. Thanks for showing me what I had. And didn't have. And had but didn't need.

Gary West and his website mrpopculture.com was an invaluable resource. I could not have written this book without the detailed '60s timeline that his site provided. How he has the time to construct this historical document I will never know.

A big thanks to Jeroen ten Berge for designing the cover and to Robert Reid and Rob Siders for their formatting.

You can always count on your fellow writers. Thanks to Tom Straw, David Isaacs, Lee Goldberg, Larry Gelbart, Lisa Messinger, Gavan Dawes, Karen Schoemer, and Treva Silverman for your terrific input and assistance.

While still protecting their anonymity a nod to several classmates from Taft High and UCLA who graciously shared their personal recollections, some way more personal than I was expecting.

And then there are the friends who were very helpful just by being there – then and now. My deepest gratitude to Howard Hoffman, Kevin Gershan, Bonnie Green, Ron Jacobs, Elizabeth Neubauer, Richard and Sara Rosenstock, Terry Abrahms, Dave Hackel, Karen Martin, Kristin Livingstone, Sophie Pustil, Ken Justiss, Jon Wolfert, Jon Solish, and Rich Brother Robbin.

There would be no ME GENERATION… BY ME if it weren't for all of THEM.

ABOUT THE AUTHOR

KEN LEVINE is an Emmy winning writer/director/producer/ major league baseball announcer. In a career that has spanned over 30 years Ken has worked on *MASH, Cheers, Frasier, The Simpsons, Wings, Everybody Loves Raymond, Becker, Dharma & Greg*, and has co-created his own series including *Almost Perfect* starring Nancy Travis. He and his partner wrote the feature *Volunteers* starring Tom Hanks and John Candy.

Ken has also been the radio/TV play-by-play voice of the Baltimore Orioles, Seattle Mariners, and San Diego Padres, and has hosted pre-and-postgame shows for the Los Angeles Dodgers.

A book about his year in Baltimore was published by Villard in 1993 entitled *It's Gone...No, Wait A Minute*.

And a book of his humorous travelogues, *Where the Hell Am I?* (http://amzn.to/HnOsdX) *Trips I Have Survived* is available in paperback or ebook on Amazon.com.

In 2011 Ken returned to the Seattle Mariners where he again does play-by-play. His blog, http://kenlevine.blogspot.com/ was named "One of the Top 25 Blogs on the Internet" by *Time* Magazine.

CPSIA information can be obtained at www.ICGtesting.com
Printed in the USA
BVOW042137191212

308741BV00001B/31/P